To Professor S. T. Bindoff
with the most sincere gratitude
and appreciation

William S. Maltby

THE BLACK LEGEND IN ENGLAND

Duke Historical Publications

THE BLACK LEGEND IN ENGLAND

The development of anti-Spanish sentiment, 1558-1660 · William S. Maltby

DUKE UNIVERSITY PRESS · DURHAM, N. C. · 1971

©1968, 1971, Duke University Press

Library of Congress Catalogue card no. 78-161356

I.S.B.N. 0-8223-0250-0

PRINTED IN THE UNITED STATES OF AMERICA BY HERITAGE PRINTERS

PREFACE

This study is the product of a long and deep-rooted interest in the development of anti-Spanish attitudes in the English-speaking world. Like many other Americans, I had imbibed anti-Hispanism from films and popular literature long before this prejudice was confirmed by my school teachers. The discovery of an entirely different viewpoint in the works of serious historians came, therefore, as something of a surprise. Though many retained a decided anti-Spanish bias, others, like Garrett Mattingly and his great predecessor Roger Bigelow Merriman, had painted a more balanced picture without sacrificing historical accuracy.

It was in this way that I became aware of the Black Legend before I learned its name, and when, as a graduate student at Duke University, I was introduced to the writings of the Hispanists, my curiosity was thoroughly aroused. Though these writers had established the existence of such a legend, their explanations of its origins seemed to raise more questions than answers. I wanted to know how anti-Spanish feeling originally developed, why it seemed so persistent and so widespread, and whether or not it had been strong enough to exert a demonstrable influence on historical events. This book is an attempt to deal with these questions by answering them within the compass of a single country and a single century. It is to be hoped that, however narrow its scope, its conclusions will afford an insight into the development of national prejudices as a general phenomenon.

For their assistance and advice in the preparation of this book, I wish to express my deepest gratitude to Professors Arthur B. Ferguson and John Tate Lanning of Duke University, both of whom have aided in the project from its inception. I would also like to thank Professor S. T. Bindoff of Queen Mary College, University of London, for his valuable counsel on both Tudor England and the perils of research in London, and to note that this work could not have been completed without the aid of a Fulbright grant for study in England. Finally, a special note of thanks to all those kindly persons, too numerous to mention, who have provided suggestions and aided in the preparation of the manuscript.

St. Louis, Missouri: June, 1969

CONTENTS

THE BLACK LEGEND IN ENGLAND

CHAPTER I. INTRODUCTION

The existence of a Black Legend that systematically denigrates the character and achievements of the Spanish people has been recognized throughout the Hispanic world for nearly four centuries. When the great satirist, Quevedo, first called attention to the phenomenon in his *España Defendida* of 1604, he was answering charges that had already troubled his countrymen for several decades. Since that date, Spain's concern for its national reputation has diminished so little that unsympathetic non-Spaniards have professed to discover in it a species of mass paranoid delusion brought on by "isolation" from the main current of European life. There is, of course, an extensive literature on the Black Legend, but esoteric theories are not needed to explain its existence. It is an understandable reaction to the large body of opinion which actually holds that the Spanish are inferior to other Europeans in those qualities commonly regarded as civilized.

Hispanists have long attributed this prejudice to distortions of historical fact committed by the enemies of Spain, but it was Julián Juderías, a Spanish journalist, who first claimed that these distortions constituted a Black Legend when he coined the term and provided a more or less definitive statement of its meaning in 1912. Juderías was particularly incensed by the notion that Spain was the home of ignorance and bigotry, an intellectual wasteland incapable of taking its place as a modern nation.[1] He was convinced, perhaps rightly, that this belief prevailed among the European intellectuals of his own time, but in his zeal to destroy the myth of Spanish backwardness he tended to neglect another, equally important aspect of the Black Legend: the stereotype of the Spaniard himself as lecherous, deceitful, and cruel.

This heavy emphasis on Spain's cultural reputation is understandable. Juderías was an intellectual. He was also, like so many Spanish writers, prone to look toward Paris for guidance rather than toward London or Amsterdam, and his acquaintance with English popular literature must have been slight in the extreme. If this was the case, he may not have been fully aware of the more barbarous manifestations of anti-Hispanism, for England and the Netherlands are a repository of anti-Spanish feeling undiluted by any regard for intellectual pretensions. It is therefore a credit to this patriotic journalist that in spite of his restricted point of view he provided a concise and, as far as it went, admirable history of the Black Legend.

According to Juderías, the roots of anti-Hispanism are to be found in what he called "The Protestant Tradition." Beginning with the revolt of the Netherlands in the sixteenth century, such documents as the *Apologia* of William of Orange and the *Relaciones* of Antonio Pérez pictured Spain as a cruel oppressor whose enormous might was enlisted in the cause of ignorance and superstition.[2] Though both of these works were written to discredit Philip II rather than Spain, and though Juderías cited no other examples, his point was well taken. Spain's efforts as the champion of Catholicism during the sixteenth and seventeenth centuries earned the country the undying hatred of Protestants in every corner of Europe—perhaps to a degree that even the Hispanists have not fully realized. The sheer quantity of anti-Spanish material that issued from the presses of Protestant Europe during this period is astonishing, and it was ably supplemented by the work of those who, while sympathetic to the Counter-Reformation, resented Spain's power and its tendency to interfere in the affairs of France and Italy.

This was, of course, only a beginning. The writers of the Enlightenment, in their battle against superstition and bigotry, saw Spain as an ideal target for their barbs. People like Raynal, Marmontel, Roucher, and DePauw seized eagerly on the testimony of the Protestants and revived the tales of Bartolomé de Las Casas to prove that Spain and barbarism were very nearly synonymous.[3] Their rediscovery of Las Casas, who had written a passionate sixteenth-century indictment of Spanish cruelties in the New World, is particularly interesting as it added an element to the Black Legend which has been heavily emphasized by later Hispanists. But Juderías rightly preferred to concentrate on their argument that Spain, the land of the Inquisition and orthodoxy, stood as an unsurpassed example of the evils of clericalism. He felt that this carefully fostered impression accounted for the nineteenth century liberal's antipathy to his native land, and for the outpouring of liberal wrath when Spain, after ridding itself of Napoleanic troops, appeared to divest itself of French ideals as well.[4] He concluded his volume by accusing certain historians of his own day, notably Lea, Pirenne, and Motley, of anti-Hispanism, and noting the influence of the Spanish-American War in bringing the Black Legend to the United States.[5]

Sound though the general outline of this argument may be, it has not been permitted to rest without further comment. The writers who have dealt in one way or another with the Black Legend are far too numerous to mention here, but certain contributions have been important enough to warrant further discussion. Among these is the work of Rómulo Cárbia, an Argentine historian whose *Historia de la Leyenda Negra Hispano-Americana* (Buenos Aires, 1943) discussed the development of anti-Hispanism in Latin America during the wars of independence, and dealt at some length with the influence of Las Casas.

More radical were the writings of Sverker Arnoldsson, who rejected the theories of Juderías in favor of an original interpretation of his own. The Black Legend was, in his view, far older than anyone had imagined. Its origins lay in the early days of the Italian Renaissance when the activities of Catalan merchants and Aragonese princes aroused resentment throughout Italy.[6] Without citing specific sources, he noted that the "pre-Renaissance humanists" stigmatized their Spanish acquaintances as *"rudos, ignorantes, sin intereses intelectuales,"*[7] and argued, far more convincingly, that Spanish behavior during the sixteenth century did little to erase this impression. The struggle for Naples and the atrocities committed at Rome in 1527 unquestionably contributed to anti-Hispanism in Italy, as did the introduction of alien Spanish customs and fashion. Even Arnoldsson's discovery of a Black Legend in Germany beginning with *"la ocupación de este país por tropas de la Península"* during the Schmalkaldic Wars is not without warrant,[8] though the reference to this relatively small force as an "occupation" is perhaps exaggerated.

All of these works, and this is but a small sample of those written on the Black Legend, have added greatly to our understanding of the phenomenon. They have defined it and, to some extent, located its sources, but they have at the same time neglected to trace its development in England. This is doubly unfortunate, not only because anti-Spanish feeling has been strong in the Anglo-Saxon countries, but because the English Black Legend possesses some unique features which are rarely encountered elsewhere. For one thing, the English have shown little interest in criticizing Spanish intellectual standards. Instead, they have created a formidable stereotype of the Spaniard himself which comprises most of the vices and shortcomings known to man. Readers of Anglo-Saxon historical novels are all too familiar with its general outline. When the Spaniard has the upper hand, his cruelty and hauteur are unsupportable. When reduced to his proper stature by some unimpeachably nordic hero, he is cringing and mean-spirited, a coward whose love of plots and treacheries is exceeded only by his incompetence in carrying them out.[9]

In many ways, the continued existence of this stereotype in the English-speaking world is an anachronism. The United States has long possessed a Spanish literary tradition, and there have always been ample numbers of Englishmen and Americans who are fascinated by Spain, and who are prepared, if necessary, to defend its reputation. The traditional view of Spain's historical role has been modified to some extent by serious historians, and every summer finds thousands of British and American tourists descending upon the Iberian Peninsula in search of sun and Culture at reduced prices. All of this has undoubtedly produced a heightened respect for Spain and its people, but to a remarkable degree this respect has not yet been reflected in films, textbooks, or popular literature.[10]

The suspicion naturally arises that such a paradox has been nourished on the continued inability of some reputable teachers and historians to rid themselves of their own anti-Spanish prejudices. The magnitude of this problem may be seen in a random selection of history texts currently being used in American high schools. "First he [Cortés] doublecrossed the governor of Cuba, then he doublecrossed the emperor Moctezuma. The Emperor had welcomed the Spaniards as descendants of the god Quetzalcoatl. His reward was imprisonment by Cortés."[11] This, according to one author, is all that American high school students need to know about the conquest of Mexico. Three centuries of Spanish activity in the New World are dismissed with the comment that a "thirst for gold" prevented serious development, and that even this treasure was "squandered" by the feckless Spaniards.[12] The authors of another text were so impressed with this theme that their entire chapter on Spanish colonial efforts is entitled "The Thirst for Gold,"[13] while yet another author concludes his presentation with the following topic for class discussion: "Name," says he, "some men in recent times who have tried to gain power by ruthless means."[14]

For those students to whom a textbook represents the full embodiment of historical truth, these misconceptions may forever remain uncorrected, but even those fortunate enough to advance beyond this level will encounter other examples of the same sentiment penned by far more formidable writers over the past four hundred years and published in every corner of the English-speaking world.

If this is the case, why has the Black Legend been so neglected by English scholars? Perhaps the answer lies in a fallacy common to nearly every work written on the subject: the idea that worldwide anti-Hispanism has but a single point of origin. In this view, the Legend is seen as a great tree whose taproot is found in a specific historical event as reported by someone like Las Casas or William of Orange. Its branches spring from the efforts of lesser men who, having read the original, were in some way inspired to improve upon it. All too often, the source of this subsidiary inspiration remains undisclosed, as does the existence of a thriving anti-Spanish literature long before the writings in question were published.

The work of Sverker Arnoldsson may once again be cited as an example. Though willing to acknowledge the historical origins of anti-Hispanism, he emphasized one group of sources at the expense of others, basing his selection on the seductive principle of chronology. Thus he states flatly that the Black Legend is of Italian origin on the grounds that anti-Spanish writings seem to have appeared there earlier than anywhere else.[15] This may well be true, but such a statement does not explain how the feelings of the Italians were transmitted to the rest of Europe. While Spanish activities were no doubt resented by many, the two Italian historians best known to Elizabethan England provided little evidence of the fact. Machiavelli, perhaps the most famous of them, was little interested in the relative merits of Italy's invaders, but his praise for Ferdinand of

Aragon is of the highest order.[16] Most of the examples from which *The Prince* is drawn are, of course, classical, and the *History of Florence* ends before the beginning of Spanish influence. There is no discernible anti-Hispanism in either.

Guicciardini, who did deal with the period of Spanish influence, requires a more careful examination. His *Storia d'Italia*, translated by Geoffrey Fenton as *The Historie of Guicciardin, conteining the warres of Italy*, went through three English editions in 1579, 1599, and 1618, a popularity justified no less by its objectivity than by its literary merits. Though the partition of Naples, as he described it, will never excite the admiration of moralists, he praises the Spanish soldiers for their courage, tenacity, and ability to endure "long travels and perplexities."[17] He invariably refers to their leader, Gonsalo de Córdoba, as "the Great Captain" and almost exonerates the Spaniards involved in the Sack of Rome by placing the major blame for this atrocity on the German *Landesknechten*.[18]

Let us admit that England is not the sole touchstone for evidence of the Black Legend, but let us also recognize that the Italians could not have been responsible for the anti-Hispanism that flourished there in the sixteenth and seventeenth centuries. Obviously, the origins of this feeling were multiple. Several nations, Italy and England among them, reacted unfavorably to a number of Spanish activities, and their attitudes were fortified when similar reactions became known through the process of cultural interchange. Only with the passage of time were they fused into the worldwide Black Legend of today, and then only incompletely. Arnoldsson, of course, was not unaware of this, but by emphasizing one point of origin to the exclusion of others he tended to foster an oversimplification. The present study, which also concentrates on the efforts of a single nation, may be partly open to the same criticism. Why then was it undertaken?

National stereotypes are a very real and disturbing component of the world in which we live. They are an essential part of national consciousness, and of that nationalism whose offspring have included two world wars and a shoal of tiny and embittered petty states, few of which are capable of supporting their own populations. Under the circumstances, it would seem that this phenomenon is worth investigating. The fact that no such task has been attempted until now is a tribute to the difficulties involved. Nothing is so hard to uncover as the private beliefs of a generation four centuries dead, and nothing is so hard to trace as the influence of these beliefs on subsequent history. In order to cope with such a problem at all, it is necessary to isolate a single national prejudice and follow it from its beginnings in a series of historical events to the first of its discernible results. Hopefully, it can then be used as a paradigm for understanding other such prejudices, wherever or whenever they arise.

Anti-Hispanism in England has been selected for this role because of its venerable antiquity. Formed in the days when European man was first groping toward a concept of nationhood, fueled by religious antagonisms that are not yet dead, and by an intense rivalry for overseas empire, it is a worthy prototype of hatreds that are developing in our own time. Moreover, the career of Anglo-Saxon anti-Hispanism has been fascinating in its own right. The "Black Legend" has undeniably played a large part in the troubled relations between the United States and its Spanish-speaking neighbors, and it continues to influence British policies with regard to Spain. However difficult it may be to isolate, it remains a factor in international affairs.

For Americans, the study of a national prejudice possesses an even deeper interest. In more ways than one, the position of the United States in the twentieth century approximates that of Spain in the sixteenth. Wielding enormous power in the defense of an essentially conservative ideal, it finds itself the object of hatred and jealousy to friends and foes alike. No one who reads the newspapers can doubt that a new Black Legend is being assembled by the nations of the world, or that America is the intended victim. Like Spain, the United States has enjoyed world power. Like Spain, it has indulged its passion for self-criticism to the fullest; and in the end, its fate may be the same. America too may live to see its glories forgotten and its proudest achievements discredited by the polemical talents of its enemies.

For those whose modesty and common sense forbid them to indulge in such speculations, this subject possesses a less controversial feature of interest. It was inevitable that in tracing the development of a national stereotype, some attention would have to be given to the way in which public opinion was formed. Though historians have lately become interested in Tudor "propaganda," no one, to my knowledge, has attempted to survey the treatment of a single large subject in the popular press. It is now possible to discover not only what was said about Spain, but who said it and, in many cases, why. In retrospect, this has been the most difficult part of the task, for little is known of the men who produced the pamphlets, broadsides, and popular histories that comprise so much of England's literary output between 1558 and 1660. Freedom of the press had not yet been invented, and those who commited political thoughts to paper were well advised to remain anonymous. Thus, while the quest has not been entirely successful, it is hoped that it will provide some new insights into English popular literature and the halting attempts of three successive rules to control its content.

In order to achieve these objectives it has been necessary to rely heavily on literary sources. Though the evidence has arrayed itself without difficulty on the framework of historical events, some words of caution are still in order. We must insist that even the most virulent anti-Spanish writings were penned by individuals in response to specific historical events, and that the occasions on which they were subsequently recalled tended to be very much like those which had inspired them in the first place. For this reason it has been necessary to organize this study around the events themselves, rather than around the character or nationality of the writers. Then we must remember that the written word not only influences popular opinion but reflects it as well. Without reviving the chicken and egg controversy, it would be well to note that the men we are dealing with fulfilled much the same function as a modern journalist. Their economic survival depended upon a basic sympathy with the prejudices of their readers or with those of some powerful patron. While their literary efforts may have influenced the waverers, they are also proof that a strong body of opinion could draw its own conclusions from such events as the Armada.

One final point. The Black Legend may not constitute a legitimate or justifiable point of view, but it is necessary to recall that it is a legend and not a myth. It sprang, as legends do, from actual events, and these cannot be ignored in the interests of partisanship. Spaniards committed grave wrongs, but so did men of other nations; and a comparative study of national crimes, while it might prove illuminating, is quite simply impossible. Though this study will demonstrate that Spain's misdeeds were exaggerated by its enemies, and that these enemies have themselves proved guilty of similar enormities, its purpose lies neither in a comparison of national morals nor in a vindication of the Spanish character. Rather, it seeks to determine how and why Spain's reputation fell victim to the sustained malice of its enemies and, by examining the Black Legend in England during the first century of its existence, to attain a more complete understanding of all such phenomena.

CHAPTER II. THE TEARS OF THE INDIANS

Anti-Hispanism in England was a native growth, but even had it been otherwise, the non-English writers mentioned by Juderías, Cárbia, and Arnoldsson could scarcely have initiated the movement by themselves. The translation of their works into English came, for the most part, too late in the sixteenth century to be decisive, but in spite of this, their efforts were not entirely barren. Once introduced, their writings quickly became known and appreciated by a people whose susceptibility to foreign influence was at that time proverbial. Drayton's comment that "the English apes and very zanies be / Of everything that they do hear or see" expressed a truth which might disturb the ardent patriot, but which augured well for the pedlar of foreign wares, literary or otherwise. Writing with verve and skill, many of these foreigners found a receptive audience and a permanent place among the founders of literary anti-Hispanism. As most of them were Spaniards, their contributions were often unintentional, though of great importance nonetheless. They provided a treasure chest of anti-Spanish stories which could be opened whenever the occasion demanded; and it was only in their pages that the English reader could learn of the Spanish conquests in the New World.

The most famous of these authors was Bartolomé de Las Casas, the Dominican friar who became Bishop of Chiapas. His *Brevissima Relación de la Destrucción de las Indias* has been widely celebrated as a cornerstone of the Black Legend and discussed at such length that Professor Hanke has warned against spreading its accusations by quoting them too freely.[1] The fact that its author was as Spanish as the men he so heartily condemned lent a dramatic touch of irony, and from another point of view, verisimilitude, to his charges. If Spaniards spoke so ill of one another, the English could scarcely be blamed for doing likewise! Internal criticism, however constructive, was rarely tolerated in Elizabethan or Stuart England, and it was hard for men to believe that absolute monarchs like Charles V and Philip II encouraged it among their subjects. Apart from matters of faith, freedom of speech was a cherished Spanish prerogative during the Golden Age, and it was not suffered to lapse through disuse. Powerful indictments of a wide range of evils were the result, and some of these, like the *Brevissima Relación*, could later be used as anti-Spanish propaganda.

The influence of Las Casas is to be found in a variety of English writings, and versions of his work have never lacked buyers. As late as 1898, a rather fanciful translation of the text was printed in New York as propaganda for the Spanish-American War, but the English-speaking world had been apprised of its contents since the publication of *The Spanish Colonie, or Brief Chronicle of the Actes and Gestes of the Spaniards in the West Indies* in 1583. Within a year, Richard Hakluyt referred to it in his *Discourse concerning Western Planting*, thereby becoming the first of many English writers who used it for purposes ranging from diatribe to sincere scholarship. Among those who confessed their debt were Raleigh, Thomas Gage, and Daniel Neal, but the historical and pamphleteering literature of the sixteenth and seventeenth centuries contains many more references that could only have come from this source. The need for a wider acquaintance with the work was partially filled by Samuel Purchas, who condensed it in *Purchas, His Pilgrimes* as an accompaniment to the Cadiz expedition of 1625. The timing may have been coincidental, but Las Casas has always had a way of reappearing during conflicts with Spain. In 1656, while Cromwell's troops were busying themselves about the "Western Design" in Jamaica, a definitive translation by John Phillips appeared to fortify the righteous indignation of his Puritan neighbors. Dramatically entitled *The Tears of the Indians*, it went through a second edition in 1699.

This popularity forces us to examine the origins of the work, for like so many controversial writings it was intended as a specific response to a specific situation. The discovery and conquest of vast areas in the New World had brought Spain face to face with a problem of unprecedented magnitude: how to deal with vast numbers of newly acquired subjects whose cultures not only were alien to European experience but differed widely even among themselves. To many Spaniards, as to adventurers the world over, simple exploitation was the answer; but to others, motivated by Christian principles or simple common sense, such courses seemed both immoral and self-defeating. Though at one time an exploiter in his own right, Las Casas was converted to the latter point of view by the sermons of

Montesinos and set forth with all the zeal of a convert on the course which was to earn him the title, "Apostle to the Indians." For the next fifty years of his extraordinary life, he waged a surprisingly effective battle against Spanish abuses in the Indies, but most particularly against those of the *encomienda* system.

Owing chiefly to the lack of extensive documentation, invective and controversy have obscured the true nature of this institution. The Spanish Crown, faced with the threefold problem of rewarding its *conquistadores*, providing revenue for itself, and "civilizing" the Indians, arrived at a solution which would, in theory at least, have attained all three objectives with a minimum of bother and expense. As stated in the Cédula of December 20, 1503, a given number of Indians could be granted to a loyal servant for the remainder of his life, provided he did not attempt to abuse them, sell them, or pass them on to his heirs. The enslavement of Indians was prohibited, and it was hoped that the *encomendero* would provide protection and religious instruction for his charges.[2] This was no great departure from current European practice and closely resembled the system of distributing Moorish lands after the fall of Granada in 1492.[3] To modern eyes, the *encomienda* seems an illiberal anachronism, but the legal anarchy it replaced was far worse. By transporting this system to the New World, the rulers of Spain managed to inhibit the growth of an Indian slave trade and to inspire some measure of stability in an inherently chaotic situation.

This is not to say that the system was impervious to abuse or that it was ever entirely satisfactory to anyone but the *encomenderos* themselves. Throughout the first half of the sixteenth century attempts were made to modify or suppress it at the urgings of clerics like Las Casas. It is a credit to Spanish justice and administration that the pleas of such men, for the most part humble friars, were permitted not only to reach the Emperor but to exert an influence on his policy. An extensive campaign of lobbying and persuasion resulted in a series of inquiries by Crown officials, and on November 20, 1542, Charles V gave his approval to the "Laws and Ordinances newly made by His Majesty for the government of the Indies and preservation of the Indians." Among other things, these New Laws, as they were called, forbade the further extension of the *encomienda* system and required that existing *encomiendas* revert to the Crown upon the death of their holders. Furthermore, royal officials were empowered to investigate charges of cruelty and to deprive guilty *encomenderos* of their Indians.[4] Such legislation obviously aimed at the destruction of the system and, had it survived for more than three years, would have been the culminating success of Las Casas's long and active career. As it was, a rebellion nearly broke out among the *conquistadores* who objected to seeing their hard-won prosperity legislated away by stay-at-home bureaucrats. After a lengthy and acrimonious debate, the New Laws were repealed in 1545, but not before they had called forth a document which, in the interval since that distant struggle, has darkened the reputation of Spain in every corner of the civilized world. In 1542, Las Casas, trying to shock Spanish officialdom into radical corrective action, penned nine treatises advocating the cause of the oppressed Indians. One of these was the celebrated *Brevissima Relación*.

Here once again the irony of the situation is inescapable. The most powerful indictment of Spain's cruelty and avarice is at the same time a monument to its humanitarianism and sense of justice. But men of other nations, writing in the heat of religious or national partisanship, could not be expected to recognize the all-important fact that Las Casas himself was a Spaniard. It is also noteworthy that while the *Brevissima Relación* was first printed in 1551, it was not until 1583, when the growing enmity between Spain and England could no longer be disguised, that the first English language edition of the work appeared in the stalls of London booksellers. Its preface left no doubt as to the motives of its publishers. By portraying Spanish methods of dealing with subject peoples, it was hoped that the Netherlanders, then engaged in their tenacious struggle for independence, would forget their internal squabble and unite in a vigorous new offensive against the "tyranny" of Parma.[5] As the edition was printed in English rather than Dutch or French, it is safe to assume that there were other considerations involved.

The first twenty years of Elizabeth's reign had seen a steady accumulation of political tension in Europe. With Parma's veterans facing them across the Channel and reports of distant sea battles ringing in their ears, many Englishmen felt that serious trouble lay ahead and that their countrymen should be mentally prepared for it. Then as now, such preparation consisted of arousing popular hatred against the potential enemy; a task to which the *Brevissima Relación* was admirably suited. Though not particularly long as books go, Las Casas's treatise contained most of the elements of the Black Legend. He seems to have thought of the pre-Columbian Indians as living in a state of nature, "without malice or subtlety," a golden age whose primal innocence was shattered forever by the coming of the Spaniard.[6] In a passage which set the tone for the whole work, he vividly presented his accusations:

> The Spaniards with their horses, their spears, and their lances, began to commit murders and strange cruelties. They entered into Towns, Boroughs, and Villages, sparing neither women with child, neither them that layed in, but that they ripped their bellies, and cut them in pieces, as if they had been opening of lambs shut up in their fold. They layed wagers with such as with one thrust of a sword could paunch or bowel a man in the middest, or with one blow of the sword should most readily and deliverly cut off his head, or that would best pierce his entrails at one stroke. They took little souls by the heels, ramping them from their mother's dugs, and crushing their heads against the cliffs. Others they cast into the river laughing and mocking, and when they tumbled in the water they said, now shift for thyself, such a one's corpse. They put others together with their mothers and all they met to the edge of the sword. They made certain Gibbets long and low, in such sort, that the foot of the hanged touched in a manner the ground, every one enough for thirteen in honor and worship of our Saviour and his twelve Apostles (as they used to speak) and setting to fire burned them all quick that were fastened.[7]

No reason or explanation is given for these insensate acts of cruelty; but at other times, Las Casas indicated that such atrocities were usually the result, if not of policy, of convenience!

Incredible as this last excuse may sound, the good Bishop had an even more incredible tale with which to support it. Its origin was admittedly obscure, and he himself was not certain where or when the incident took place, but he told it anyway and thereby provided later writers with one of their most popular libels. In Yucatan, or perhaps it was New Spain, a Spaniard went hunting with his dogs.

Coming upon an Indian woman and her baby, he noticed that the beasts were hungry, and tearing the child from its mother's arms, fed it piecemeal to his hounds.[8] The creatures must surely have been famished to accept such a dish, but even stranger than their exotic tastes is the fact that such an extraordinary story should be so indefinite in detail. Be that as it may, the rules of evidence acceptable to public opinion have always been lax, and the Spaniards who fed children to their dogs have not been forgotten.

Such incidents, whatever their validity, need not have been taken as proof of national depravity, nor would they have been had Las Casas not regarded them as part of a larger program of atrocity. The famed "massacre of Cholula" may be cited as a case in point. According to Las Casas, it was Cortés's policy of awing the natives into submission that resulted in the slaughter,[9] but other writers, including those present at the affair, saw matters differently. Gómara, the "official" historian of the expedition, claimed that Cortés was simply forestalling a murderous plot concocted by the Cholulan nobility,[10] and Bernal Díaz did not see fit to contradict him.[11] Such an interpretation places Spanish cruelties in an entirely different light. It must be remembered that Cortés was invading a vast and far from innocent empire at the head of a mere handful of troops. His enterprise could be successful only if moral niceties were occasionally dispensed with—a fact which even English explorers came to appreciate in similar situations.

It was this same isolation that led to the employment of Indian auxiliaries—a practice fraught with embarrassment, as the English discovered during the American Revolution. As might be expected, the behavior of these "innocent children" afforded Las Casas another occasion for horrified comment. It seems that, as food was scarce during the Guatemalan campaign, the Spaniards permitted their allies to feast upon the bodies of captured hostiles, and even caused a "sort of shambles" to be set up for their convenience.[12] There is probably some truth in this statement, for many of the "noble savages" employed by the Spaniards were unquestionably cannibals, and in the general confusion following a great battle it would have been difficult, and perhaps dangerous, to restrain their propensity for human flesh. To suggest that they needed or received help in butchering their victims is of course another matter. We can only conclude that once again Las Casas's commitment to charity was overriding truth.

Such failures of historical imagination in dealing with the moral problems of the Conquest need not be wondered at. Equivocation has never been desirable in clerics, and Las Casas, as the voice of conscience, was honor bound to speak plainly. On the other hand, his more blatant exaggerations can be explained only in terms of the polemicist's art. His allegation that anywhere from thirty to fifty million Indians were slain by the Spaniards is patently absurd and has justly exposed him to much ridicule and indignant reproach. Though it is generally agreed that Indians died or were slain in great numbers during the early years of Spanish rule, it is also agreed that the entire native population of New Spain would not have equaled the numbers slain in the *Brevissima Relación*.[13] Spain's record of cruelty is unenviable, but unlike the Puritans of New England, Spain never favored a policy of deliberate extermination, and its cruelties were those that have ever accompanied empire-building. New lands are rarely conquered by the meek and gentle, and the Spanish colonies were no exception to this rule.

Had Las Casas been asked to account for this violence, his answer would no doubt have been different. Throughout his book, greed plays counterpoint to atrocity, and it is likely that, had he been interested in motives, avarice would have headed the list. Reports of unjust exactions and of Indians being worked to death are too numerous to recount; but one story, combining poignancy with a certain grim humor, serves as an illustration of his main point—that greed and brutality were hindering the all-important work of conversion. When the *conquistadores* first invaded Hispaniola, an Indian chieftain with the improbable name of Hathvey took refuge on the neighboring island of Cuba. Before long his dreams of security proved mere delusions, for the Spaniards, not content with the devastation they had wrought upon his homeland, were seen to approach Cuba as well. Upon hearing this terrible news, Hathvey gathered the local Indians together and delivered a speech. In it, he discoursed at length on the cruelties of the white man, cruelties which he said proceeded from the worship of a "covetous and unsatisfied" deity. At this point, he held up a small chest of gold. Calling this the god of the Spaniards, he urged his audience to appease it with dancing and singing, following which it was to be cast into the river, lest the Spaniards come and kill them for it.[14]

Las Casas undoubtedly hoped that by including such a tale he would properly horrify his countrymen, whom he probably suspected of being more orthodox than humanitarian. In so doing he may have calculated well, for whatever the shortcomings of their administration, no other nation equaled the Spanish in their concern for the souls of new subjects. Nowhere was there such piety of official intention, such lengthy and learned deliberation on how the Indian's salvation might best be achieved; nor, in the last analysis, was any nation so successful in grafting its religion onto an alien culture. But as a cleric, Las Casas did not consider this progress satisfactory. One of his major complaints, best enunciated in a sort of peroration to the *Brevissima Relación*, remained that the Spaniards, for all their pretense of evangelical fervor, had done nothing to care for heathen souls.[15] Only once does he refer to the labors of the friars,[16] leading the reader to suppose that his silence betokens a religious vacuum when in reality the numerous recorded instances of ecclesiastical courage and idealism reveal an entirely different situation.

His distortions and exaggerations, only a few of which have been mentioned here, are, in other words, so serious as to cast doubt on his entire thesis. That they have not generally done so is a tribute not merely to the bigotry of his foreign readers but to an element of truth which his writings, like most polemics, undoubtedly possess. Sir Arthur Helps was making a fool of himself when he said, "I have not the slightest doubt of the truth of any statement that he thus vouches for,"[17] but his naiveté was little greater than that of certain Spaniards, who reject Las Casas root and branch because he lies occasionally. The men who first planted the flag of Spain in the New World were not always drawn from the most respectable elements of society; nor was their position, once they arrived, one to encourage morality where there had been none before. Constant danger combined with an absence of effective authority brings out the worst in men, and the conduct of many *conquistadores* remains a blot upon Spanish arms. We must conclude, as Lewis Hanke does, that "no one today would defend the statistics Las Casas gave, but few would deny that there was considerable truth in his main charges."[18] The fact that similar acts occurred whenever Europeans found themselves in contact with weak or unmilitary peoples reflects upon the veracity of the Black Legend, not of Las Casas. He argued that cruel and barbarous men were engaged in the colonization of America and that their worst excesses should be legally curbed. It was his English translator who decided that the Spanish were an exceptionally "cruel and barbarous nation."[19] But then he could not have lived to see the tales of Las Casas reenacted in the colonies of other nations including his own. The *conquistadores* were often appalling, but there is little to suggest that their conduct was unique.

This fine distinction would necessarily have escaped an Elizabethan Englishman who saw Spain as a threat to his home and religion. He was prepared to believe the worst, and the *Brevissima Relación* fortified his prejudice. Circumstances would have produced a Black Legend without Las Casas, but he, a Spaniard, contributed mightily to its form and content.

Corroboration of his charges came from an unexpected and, one is tempted to say, unimpeachable source: the *Crónica de la Nueva España* of Francisco López de Gómara. Written by Cortés's personal chaplain and translated by an open admirer of Spanish exploits, this was obviously no diatribe, though it referred to several of the incidents described by Las Casas. They were related from an entirely different point of view, but armed with a new certainty as to time and place, the English reader could feel that his bias was justifiably reinforced. Thomas Nicholas, who translated the *Crónica* into English as *The Pleasant Historie of the Conquest of the VVest India, now called New Spayne*, appears to have been wholly unaware of this fact. In his dedication to Sir Francis Walsingham, he stated that he had undertaken the labor of translation so that Englishmen might emulate Spain, particularly in the "Northwest Territories" then being investigated by Frobisher.[20] Nicholas may not have been an Hispanophile—while an agent for the Levant Company he had been arrested by the Inquisition and freed only after five years at the personal insistence of Elizabeth[21]—but he was wise enough to respect his adversaries. When he published in 1578, popular anti-Hispanism had not yet reached the intensity of the eighties, and in his encouragement of rivalry through emulation he reflected the government's policy of competition without open war.

Consequently, the *Pleasant Historie* cannot be called a major contribution to the Black Legend. Gómara did increase the fund of Las Casan horror stories by relating how eight hundred remnants of the once proud Aztec nation were slain by the Spaniards as they foraged for scraps in the ruins of their city,[22] but his real importance lies in the subordinate role of attesting, however unwittingly, to the exaggerations of Las Casas.

Another of Nicholas's translations, *The Strange and Delectable History of the discouerie and Conquest of Peru*, is not quite so innocuous. Its author, Augustín de Zárate, had gone out to Peru as *contador de mercedes* in the *Audiencia* of Blasco Nuñez Vela and was therefore an eyewitness to many of the scenes he described. Though proud of his countrymen's exploits and notably unsympathetic to the Indians, Zárate, like many another in those dark days following the Conquest, was led by partisanship to reveal what others might have left unsaid. By the time he arrived, the conquerors of the Incas had fallen to fighting over the spoils, and the bitter strife between the Pizarro and Almagro factions provided many an incident guaranteed to bring comfort to Hispanophobes everywhere. In vehemently supporting Francisco Pizarro, Zárate castigated his enemies so thoroughly that he cast doubts on the Spanish character as a whole, though unlike the "Apostle to the Indians" he reserved his indignation for crimes committed by the Spaniards against their fellows. Like many of Las Casas's opponents, he regarded the Indians as little more than beasts, given over entirely to perversion and human sacrifice.[23] He refers often to the cruelty and insolence of the native rulers and, while giving much attention to native customs, leaves no doubt that he regarded the coming of Spain, the Almagros included, as a distinct improvement over former conditions. His very callousness, which calls to mind the Anglo-Saxon saying that "the only good Indian is a dead Indian," allowed him to include episodes which a hostile reader might seize upon with glee. One such tale finds Diego Almagro the Elder burning a cacique for running

away from him. The marginal comment reads simply and characteristically, "Justice,"[24] but the English reader might thereby be ex-
cused for wondering at the state of Spanish jurisprudence.

Almagro and the other *conquistadores* did not, of course, confine
their barbarities to the Indians but practiced them upon one another
with a fine impartiality that aroused Zárate's ire. Admittedly, the
execution of Almagro the Elder is not regarded with the same indignation as the murder of Francisco Pizarro, but looking at it from
Zárate's point of view, the former had "exalted himself in pride" and
"shown some bitterness of cruelty" toward the Pizarros:[25] crimes
that undoubtedly entitled him to just retribution. Under the circumstances, his son's bloody revenge could be described only as "treachery and insolence."[26] These unsavory doings are in themselves sufficient to blacken the Spanish character, but they are compounded
with an accusation, rare in the sixteenth century, of cowardice on
the part of a Spanish soldier. Diego Almagro the Elder, *conquistador*
and scourge of the Indians, is shown grovelling on his knees before
Hernán Pizarro that his life might be spared.[27] Described with all
the relish of bitter factionalism, this scene trails an odor that is little
diminished by Zárate's fulsome praise of the Pizarros.

It is therefore doubly unfortunate that even this praise was quali-
fied. Zárate seems to have been inordinately bilious even for a *contador de mercedes*, but in his personal dislike for Gonsalo Pizarro,
he plumbed new depths of rancor. When Orellana, for example, deserted Gonsalo on the Amazon expedition Zárate defended the mu-
tineers out of malice, but honesty compelled him to note a significant
and discreditable fact: the boat with which Orellana and his men
absconded happened to contain the expedition's money![28]

In other words, the author not only managed to incriminate both
sides thoroughly but to reintroduce Las Casas's charge of avarice, a
grievance already raised in his account of the Inca's death. According to Zárate, this famous murder was prompted by the Almagros,
who feared that as long as the Emperor lived all treasure would be
appropriated by the Pizarros as his ransom. As the ransom had been
agreed upon before Almagro arrived, he was entitled to none of it,
and his troops could not logically expect to share in the spoils until
it had been paid, or until the captive was dead. As this second alter-

native was the more easily accomplished, the Inca's execution was secured by implicating him in a nonexistent plot to overthrow the Spaniards.[29] As if this were not enough, the historian soon turned to open denunciation of the greed that must have made his official life a burden to him. The tensions between Pizarro's veterans and Almagro's newcomers finally culminated in the battle of Salinas, at which the latter were soundly defeated. Realizing the need for unity in the face of a possible Indian rebellion, Hernán Pizarro attempted to conciliate his late enemies with gifts and honors. These efforts were unsuccessful, "for each of them did think, that if all the government had been given him, yet this payment was not sufficient."[30]

The damage done by Zárate and Las Casas was, of course, basically unintentional. Motivated by ideals or partisanship, they besmirched Spain's reputation, as it were, in passing. Given an agitated state of public opinion, others proved that they could do almost as much in the interest of historical accuracy. Among them, Peter Martyr d'Anghiera takes pride of place.

An Italian humanist who lived in Spain during the early years of the Conquest, he was fascinated by this contact with cultures hitherto unknown and unsuspected. His elegant Latin epistles directed to influential friends at Rome provided one of the first and most valuable contemporary accounts of Spain's activities in the New World. Compiled into the book *De Orbe Novo*, they were attracting attention in faraway England by 1555. In that year Richard Eden translated and published the first three *Decades* together with a prologue that left no doubt as to his feelings. "The kings of Spain," said he, ". . . are more deserving of the name of hero than those men of antiquity who are generally accounted such,"[31] for in "enlarging the Christian world" they have set an example for all nations.[32] Thus, only three years after the *Brevissima Relación* first appeared in Madrid, an Englishman could say of the Indians:

Their bondage [under the Spanish] is such as is much rather to be desired than their former liberty which was to the cruel cannibals rather a horrible licentiousness than a liberty, and to the innocent so terrible a bondage, that in the midst of their fearful idleness, they were ever in danger to be a prey to these manhunting wolves. But the Spaniards as ministers of grace and liberty, brought unto these new gentiles the victory of Christ's death whereby they being subdued by the worldly sword, are now made free from the bondage of Satan's tyranny.[33]

Written while Philip and Mary were on the throne of a nominally Catholic England, such unqualified praise belies the claims of those who would disassociate anti-Hispanism from political conditions. What was regarded as piety in 1555 had become wickedness in 1588, and we may be sure that this transformation was not entirely due to moral progress.

In all fairness, it should be said that Martyr himself, though no enemy of Spain, was far less enthusiastic than his English translator. He tells, for example, of a massacre in which only six infants were left alive,[34] and characterizes Roldán and his men as "a filthy sink of rebels" for their mutiny against Columbus.[35] This last incident is typical of the unseemly broils that disfigured the Spanish Conquest, and there is no way in which it could have been presented creditably. Availing themselves of the unquestioned right to appeal directly to the Crown, both sides filled the air with bitter recriminations. Roldán and his followers, as Martyr faithfully reported, accused the Admiral of torturing them and of "delighting in Spanish blood," whereupon the great explorer denounced them as rebels whose insolence, laziness, and immorality were jeopardizing the whole enterprise.[36]

Martyr did not find this too surprising, nor did he believe that the turmoil arose from any perversity peculiar to Spaniards. Rather, he realized that the more respectable of men do not often find it necessary to seek their fortunes in the wilderness:

For that kind of men (the Spaniards, I mean, which followed the Admiral in that navigation) was for the most part unruly, regarding nothing but idleness, play, and liberty: And would by no means abstain from injuries: Ravishing the women of the Islands before the faces of their husbands, fathers, and brethren: by which abominable misbehaviour, they disquieted the minds of all the inhabitants.[37]

Such passages as this might have explained a lot to those prepared to listen, but taken out of context they sound remarkably like Las Casas.

Even more Las Casan was his discourse on the Spaniard's dogs which, then as now, were used as a means of controlling mobs. Las Casas the humanitarian had objected strenuously to this employment of "man's best friend," but Martyr the humanist did not. As this is a charge which appears throughout the literature of anti-Hispanism, the Italian's personal feelings are not as important as the fact that he supports it, but they do give his reporting a distinct flavor of its own. This individuality lies in his description of dogs used not in warfare but as agents of punishment and reflects something of an age that preferred retribution to rehabilitation. Vasco Núñez de Balboa, leading his expedition across the Isthmus of Panama, came upon a native ruler whose household was given over to the practice of homosexuality, a vice which Martyr held to be as repugnant to the Spaniards as it was common among the Indians.[38] Balboa, with characteristic directness, set his dogs on the lot of them, killing the chief and about forty of his *mignons*. His subjects, who thought the perversion an offense against their gods, were delighted, and Martyr adds darkly that he wished all men thought so.[39]

This story illustrates, if nothing else, the dangers involved in assessing the impact of any given incident on a sixteenth-century reader, who might, like some moderns, think the chief and his friends well served. On the other hand, it shows the ambiguity peculiar to Martyr and to the Italian historians generally—a certain bemused detachment that might mix praise with blame, or eschew both. Nowhere does he actually comment on the moral rectitude of Balboa's judgment, though he obviously has little sympathy for the pederastic Indians. It is therefore almost unfair to mention him among the founders of the Black Legend. He presented little more than the truth, but though the truth was, as usual, impartial, his readers were not; and he left them free to select his facts according to their pleasure.

These four writers, Martyr, Gómara, Zárate, and Las Casas, have remained valuable sources of information on the Spanish Conquest. With the possible exception of Las Casas, they are still of great importance to the student and have necessarily influenced our opinion of Spain. During Elizabeth's reign they were supplemented to some extent by the gleanings of Hakluyt, but it was not until 1625 that three more Spanish accounts appeared in the collection of Samuel Purchas.

Purchas, who for reasons unknown had been given the task of finishing Hakluyt's great work, was not the equal of his master. Rather than present his sources in their pristine fullness, he condensed them in a most whimsical manner, perhaps to make room for his own lengthy and irrelevant discourses. When the fables of Las Casas were involved, this could be forgiven, but such writers as Garcilaso de la Vega deserved more considerate treatment. Purchas probably felt that as "the Inca's" work had been so extensively quoted elsewhere, a fuller treatment was unnecessary. As a result, his readers were treated to a brief abridgment, of which the most important passages, for our purposes at least, dealt with the murder of Manco the Inca and the rebellion of Tupac Amaru.

In the first case, the blame for the incident is placed squarely on the shoulders of a Spaniard named Gómez, who, in a fit of bad manners, treated the Inca as his slave. Infuriated, Manco hit him with his fist, whereupon Gómez seized a drinking bowl and struck him dead. "Thus died Manco by the hands of those whom he had preserved from death, and had kindly used."[40]

This was outright murder at the hands of a drunken ruffian, but to Garcilaso, the execution of Tupac Amaru was little better. The rebellion, as he saw it, was a myth, a legal fiction whose sole purpose was to satisfy the personal animosity of the Viceroy Toledo.[41] Tupac Amaru, a good and noble man, was therefore sentenced and executed for high treason without any particulars being named in the bill against him.[42] This interpretation of events was, of course, untrue, as the victim had declared himself to be the Inca and had attempted to rouse the Indians against their oppressors, but Garcilaso's was the only account available in English at that time. As was so often the case, Purchas had selected the worst part of an otherwise excellent work for inclusion in his book.

More circumstantial was the story of Lope de Aguirre as related by López Vaz. Set in the rain forests of the Amazon Basin, it is a tale of sheer horror unredeemed by the virtues of courage or perseverance. Lope de Aguirre was, for all his small stature and game leg, a member of Ursua's expedition and evidently, like many of his fellows, found the hard work of discovery unrewarding. At his suggestion, as seconded by a certain Don Fernando de Guzman, the soldiers decided to mutiny, kill their leader, and return to seize the province of Peru for themselves. Together with Guzman, Lope slew Ursua in his tent and then proceeded to forswear his allegiance to the King on a temporary altar set up for the purpose. Guzman was elected king in turn, but his reign proved a brief one. Angered by his refusal to abandon the women and porters, Lope killed him on the spot and secured his own position by murdering all those of gentleman's rank in the company. By the time he reached Margarita Island, he had slain 170 of the expedition's 400 members and left many more to perish at the hands of the headhunters.[43] Curiously enough, the author seems to have realized what an effect his narrative could have on the non-Spanish reader. In attempting to explain Lope's insane behaviour, he says, "(he was of the Country of Biscay, a land joining unto France, therefore I rather believe that he was a Frenchman than a Spaniard, for that in the heart of a Spaniard there is not so much cruelty as this man had)."[44]

The third of Purchas's selections was quite different from the others, and indeed from most of those he sought to preserve. Father Jerónimo Benzos, like Las Casas, was not interested in providing information on the Spanish colonies but in castigating the ill-treatment of the Indians and the laxness of the clergy. While his descriptions of tortured and overworked Indians are numerous, they are not so spectacular as his predecessor's, nor has he been so much quoted in this regard. His original contribution was a scathing denunciation of the Spanish clergy in the New World, which, together with the descriptions of secular brutality already recorded, completed the picture of a wholly depraved society.

There are monks which perpetrate those things openly by day-light, which others would be ashamed to do by night. And a Franciscan publicly preached, that there was neither Priest, nor Monk, nor Bishop in India, worthy the name of a good man. For they had given themselves to covetousness, and still went to the wealthy countries, and avoided the poorer. For these words he was apprehended, and carried to Guatemala. I have also heard Priests discoursing together, that they came out of Spain into India for gain, and nothing else.[45]

With the clergy in such a state, it was small wonder that the Indians had become lewd and immoral through their association with the Spanish.[46] Las Casas's befuddled cacique comes inevitably to mind when Benzos tells us,

> Some of them shewing a piece of Gold, will say, Lo here is the Christians God, for this they have come hither, for this they have subdued us, and done so many mischiefs, for this they are never quiet, but dice, blaspheme, curse, steal, commit rapes, and do whatsoever villainy and lust.[47]

These then were the accounts of the Spanish Conquest available to sixteenth- and seventeenth-century Englishmen. Most of them were straightforward histories whose importance to anti-Hispanism lies only in their honest refusal to disguise the more unsavory aspects of the truth. Others were polemics aimed at eradicating specific abuses, while still others, like José de Acosta's *Natural and Moral History of the Indies*, were largely concerned with other matters and mentioned the treatment of the Indians only in passing.[48] The polemicists excepted, most were willing to give the *conquistadores* and their clerical companions their due. The tales of outstanding heroism and sacrifice far outnumber those of a discreditable nature, and only Las Casas and Benzos can be called true contributors to the Black Legend.

Nevertheless, Las Casas proved the most popular of them all with the English people, as his success in publication will indicate. Caught up as they were in the struggle with Spain, most English readers would no doubt have preferred to cull from their sources those assertions that would agree with their own prejudice. There can certainly be little doubt that those who wrote on the subject at a later date rarely quoted passages in praise of Spain's achievements.

The Spanish Conquest of America has played an enormous part in the development of anti-Hispanism, but that part was largely reserved for a time and place with which this study is not concerned. For the sixteenth- and seventeenth-century Englishman there were more immediate reasons for disliking Spain, and the deeds of the Spaniards in the New World were of interest primarily as ammunition in a propaganda war that was developing from other causes.

CHAPTER III. A DARK POPISH DOMDANIEL

Living as we do in an age of relative unbelief, we are sometimes tempted to forget that our forebears were as obsessed with religious questions as we are with social ideologies and that even their most materialistic projects were apt to be justified in theological terms. The excessive number of martyrs produced during the sixteenth century forbids us to deny their sincerity completely, and, while admitting a multitude of other factors, we must recognize that religion played an important role in the development of English attitudes toward Spain.

Elizabethan England was generally regarded as the natural leader of the reformed camp, while Spain was the natural leader of the Catholics. Though possessing a large Catholic population and a Queen who was temperamentally averse to ideologies, England was one of the few European states that possessed both an established non-Roman church and the means with which to resist a revived papacy. Spain, on the other hand, was the greatest military power in the world. It possessed a strong central government and it was overwhelmingly Catholic in policy and popular sympathy: the logical champion of the Counter-Reformation and right arm of the Pope. In the pamphlet literature of the day, the Pope and the King of Spain are rarely mentioned separately. It is not surprising, then, that Spain and Catholicism came to mean much the same thing to Protestant Englishmen and that the hatred felt for the one could be applied equally to the other.

This identification of Spain with Catholicism first bore literary fruit during the reign of Philip and Mary, when men like John Bradford warned of Spanish influence in English politics.[1] Bradford naively denied that he was a Protestant and pretended to concentrate on the low moral standards of Philip's retinue, but the bulk of his tract is taken up with doctrinal arguments against the sacraments, the liturgy, and the priesthood—a clumsy attempt to turn popular distrust of strangers to the purposes of religious reform. The departure of the Spanish visitors brought an end to this kind of thing by removing the source of irritation, and for nearly a decade after Elizabeth's accession the triumphant Protestants devoted themselves to hunting "Romish foxes" on their own home ground. England and

Spain were not only at peace but united in their opposition to the French and Scots.

This happy and traditional state of affairs could not last. John Hawkins's adventures in the West Indies and the worsening situation in the Netherlands warned that the apparent cordiality masked deep and irreconcilable differences. Beginning with Hawkins's account of his fight at San Juan de Ulúa, anti-Spanish literature once more appeared in England. The smoldering religious antagonisms, hitherto checked by politics, were to be allowed free play.

The concept of Spanish Catholicism that arose in the following century was based partly on Protestant attitudes in general, and partly on certain failings thought to be uniquely Spanish. English Catholics may not have shared these views, but they were rarely in a position to oppose them. For them, publication was both difficult and dangerous. They had enough to do to defend themselves, and there is no evidence to indicate that the bulk of them were pro-Spanish to begin with. While books were occasionally published in praise of Spanish table manners or military tactics, the fact remains that in England, at any rate, the portrayal of Spanish religion was left in the hands of its worst enemies.

The results can be imagined. Spanish Catholicism was alternately disregarded as mere hypocrisy or damned as a positive encouragement to vice. Raleigh, who rarely lost an opportunity to attack Spain, said in his account of Sir Richard Grenville's death: "For matter of religion it would require a particular volume, if I should set down how irreligiously they cover their greedy and ambitious pretences with that veil of piety,"[2] while James Wadsworth, the English double agent, informed his readers that "the Spaniards were, and are, little better than Atheists, only making use of the Pope for their own particular ambitions and ends, as to confirm and establish him in unlawful monarchies, and under colour of Religion to make Subjects become Slaves."[3] More serious from the moralist's point of view were the assertions of Drake's chaplain, who claimed that "the poisonous infection of Popery" is introduced wherever the Spaniards go, and there is therefore no city, village, or house in the Indies, "wherein (amongst the other like Spanish virtues) not only whoredom, but the filthiness of Sodom, not to be named among Christians, is not common without reproof."[4] According to Raleigh's unfortunate lieutenant, Lawrence Keymis, this is true because they think themselves "well and surely blessed, however they live, if their town and houses be religiously crossed."[5]

There is nothing unfamiliar about these judgments. Similar accusations directed at the Catholic church as a whole were a staple in the sermons of the day and can still be heard in rural districts. Though they added considerable weight to the Black Legend, there is little need to examine them at length. More important were the contemporary accounts of the Spanish Inquisition, an institution which became a popular symbol of Spanish faith.

For those who are acquainted with this by no means unique organization, it is difficult to understand the morbid fascination it has exercised on so many minds. Compared to the Roman Inquisition, its methods were mild and its procedures relatively just.[6] Compared to the German witchcraft tribunals, its victims were few and its intellectual standards high. Obviously, the explanation of its fame lies elsewhere than in its severity.

Though Hispanists have usually pointed an irate finger at the eighteenth-century philosophes, there is every reason to believe that this interest dates from the revolt of the Netherlands. Faced with the task of justifying their behavior in terms acceptable to a monarchical age, the rebels argued that Philip II, though an anointed king, had overthrown their ancient privileges and instituted a religious persecution against loyal subjects. The latter point was apt to prove more acceptable in lands where the ruler, though anti-Roman, might understandably be suspicious of those who advocated limitations on a sovereign's power. Consequently, the histories and pamphlets published on the subject in England claimed with well-nigh universal accord that the states rebelled because Philip sought to introduce the Spanish Inquisition.[7] This would seem to indicate that its activities were well known and appreciated, but many of the works, particularly the earlier ones, found it necessary to describe the Inquisition and catalog its enormities!

Given the quality of these descriptions, the argument was persuasive, and its effectiveness was not marred by the fact that Philip had never intended to introduce the Inquisition at all. In a letter to

Margaret of Parma, dated July 17, 1562, the monarch said, "that which they invent concerning the Inquisition, that we wish to introduce the Spanish variety, is also false and wholly unreasonable because the one they use there is more merciless than the one here."[8] This attitude, of course, went unrevealed.

Then there were the accounts of the English voyagers. Sooner or later, those sailors unfortunate enough to be wrecked on the Spanish Main or otherwise captured by the authorities found themselves in the hands of the Inquisitors. Even traders licensed to reside in Spanish ports could fall into difficulty through some careless utterance or the malice of a competitor. If they survived, as they usually did, the reading public could expect an impassioned essay from their pens, or from a pamphleteer hired for the occasion. Some of the earliest accounts of Inquisitorial activity reached England in this way and undoubtedly served to create a deeper, more personal concern.

Together, these writings kept interest alive, but the Elizabethan concept of the purpose, organization, and methods of the Inquisition was drawn largely from two sources of an entirely different kind. The first was a curious volumne entitled *A Discovery & Plaine Declaration of sundry Subtill Practices of the Holy Inquisition of Spain* by "Reginaldus Gonsalvius Montanus." The second was John Foxe's *Book of Martyrs*.

No one really knows who Montanus was. Schäfer has suggested that he may have been one Fray Benito, a lay brother at the cloister of San Isidro in Seville, but this is admittedly no more than an educated guess.[9] It is fairly certain that whoever he was, he was in some way associated with the "Lutheran" community that was destroyed in that city during 1557–1558. The nature of this association is necessarily vague, and the uncertainty is compounded by the fact that, unlike most of the "Lutherans" of Seville, Montanus seems really to have been a Protestant. As the records of their examinations indicate, the leaders of the community were guilty of little more than Erasmian humanism,[10] yet Montanus deliberately implies throughout his book that they shared his own strongly reformed views. Bataillon maintains that in this he was at one with the Inquisitors, who made the same apparent mistake for the same reason:

both sides wished to extract the maximum propaganda value for themselves by exaggerating the importance of the case.[11]

However that may be, Montanus's book was an instantaneous success. First published in Latin at Heidelberg in 1567, it appeared in English, French, and Dutch translations the following year. Its lengthy description of Inquisitorial procedures was the first to reach England, and its account of the Seville community remains valuable in spite of its bias. The reasons for its publication are clearly stated by the English translator: it was to be a warning to England and a description of what was to be visited on the Low Countries.[12]

Foxe's work was different and, thanks to its popularity, more important. One of the Marian exiles, Foxe had fallen in with Bale and Grindal on the Continent and was soon at work latinizing the rudimentary beginnings of the latter's Protestant martyrology. The need for such a work had long been recognized by the leaders of reform, and when Grindal died Foxe was able to bring it to an impressive conclusion. The *Acts and Monuments*, commonly known as *The Book of Martyrs*, went through literally innumerable editions,[13] and soon took its place beside the Bible as the staple reading of Protestant England. The reasons for this remarkable popularity are several: the book was readable, it coincided with popular attitudes, and its historical scholarship was, on the whole, remarkably sound for the era in which it was written. The section of the book devoted to the Spanish martyrs is not large, and taken in relation to the rest of the work, it fades into insignificance. It was, in fact, an afterthought first appended to the edition of 1570 in recognition of the newly aroused in Spanish wrongdoing. Well-written, circumstantial, and timely, it has been read by people who would never have heard of Reginaldus Gonsalvius Montanus.

These two books, supplemented by the stories of English seamen and Dutch historians, provided Englishmen with their only knowledge of the Inquisition. Though biased and grossly inadequate, they presented a coherent picture of the institution that could not but influence the English conception of Spanish religion and the Spanish character. The composition of this picture is therefore worthy of examination.

Perhaps the most surprising aspect of these presentations is that they devoted considerable sympathetic attention to the history of what they were trying to condemn. Montanus in particular consumes the first several pages of his book in tracing the origins of the Inquisition in the reign of Ferdinand and Isabella. Beginning with a brief sketch of the *Reconquista*, he tells of the Moors, Jews, and *Conversos*, and of their diabolical machinations against the state. Alarmed at the malice and impiety of these people, the *Reyes Católicos* introduced the Spanish Inquisition as a check on their dangerous activities.[14] What these activities were is revealed by the anonymous author of *A Tragicall Historie of the warres in the Low Countries*. This man, whose identity defies investigation, borrowed much of his historical account from Montanus, but adds that the final decision to persecute came when the Jews crucified a child on Palm Sunday, 1475. They were, in his opinion, justly condemned, and a legalized pogrom was begun that both authors regard as praiseworthy.[15] Unfortunately, this noble work of forced conversion was perverted by the Dominicans, who gained control of the Inquisition and were now using its apparatus to enforce doctrinal uniformity among Christians. The end result was that the holy fathers exalted their own power to such heights and enforced their prejudices so rigorously that even the Spaniards had come to detest them.[16]

Though largely true, this version of the story left its readers with one or two misconceptions. As Protestants, Montanus and his anonymous successor were most concerned with the Inquisitorial function of suppressing heresy. They therefore gave the impression that the tribunal's efforts were directed at little more than rooting out dubious theological propositions. At certain times and in certain areas, this was quite correct, but the Inquisition had many other problems to deal with. In addition to their primary work of defending the Faith, the Fathers had to cope with such offenses as bigamy, blasphemy, sorcery, and solicitation in the confessional. They were also forced to undertake the censorship of books, examining them not only for heresy, but for obscenity and bad style.[17] In some jurisdictions, such as Peru, these activities counted for nearly all of the cases tried, and convictions for heresy were few.[18]

More serious was the accusation that the Inquisitors used their extraordinary powers for the furtherance of their own ends. The Dominicans were said to have used the right of confiscation to swell the coffers of their order and the Crown.[19] Foxe is quite explicit:

Three sorts of men most principally be in danger of these Inquisitors: they that be greatly rich for the spoil of their goods: they that be learned, because they will not have their misdealings and secret abuses to be espied and detected: they that begin to increase in honors, and in dignity, lest they being in authority, should work them some shame or dishonor.[20]

Once again, these statements contain an element of truth. Such flagrant abuses of power earned the Inquisition much enmity in Spain and elsewhere,[21] but Foxe's examples are not as convincing as his generalizations.

On November 5, 1560, the English merchant Nicholas Burton was visited by a familiar of the Inquisition who held him talking about commercial matters until an *alguacil* could enter and seize him. After questioning, not as to his faith but as to the location of his goods, he was sent to the common prison and held there without charge for fourteen days, following which he was taken to Seville and there burned on December 20. Foxe printed this that all might know "the extreme dealing and cruel ravening of these Catholic Inquisitors of Spain, who, under the pretended visor of religion, do nothing but seek their private gain and commodity, with crafty defrauding and spoiling of other men's goods."[22] But even Foxe was forced to admit, indirectly, that there was more in this case than met the eye. It seems that while in Cadiz jail, Burton had taken to preaching the Gospel and had even managed to convert several of his fellow inmates to Protestantism.[23] Had the Inquisitors been seeking only profit, they could not have been more fortunate in finding a man who was as heretical as he was rich.

Though this example left something to be desired, Foxe nevertheless struck a nerve. The Inquisition was notoriously addicted to confiscations, and no one could have been surprised when John Fronton, another merchant, lost his goods for omitting the final *Sancta Maria mater Dei ora pro nobis peccatoribus* in saying his Ave Maria.[24] Both of these were celebrated cases recorded not only in Foxe but in Montanus and even in Hakluyt. The best story of all, though, came from Sir Walter Raleigh, who discovered the Spaniards about to walk off with a Fleming's worldly treasures. When the poor man protested that he was a good Catholic, the rascally Iberians declared that while he himself is undoubtedly of the True Faith, his goods are heretic and subject to confiscation![25]

Such suspicions of the Inquisitors' good faith were engendered by the triviality of many heavily punished offenses. So great was the impression thus created that the Inquisitors were accused of manufacturing crimes to satisfy their sadistic desires.[26] Though Fronton's omission could hardly have been unintentional, it was certainly a minor offense, and cases like his were numerous. At other times, the Inquisitors were said to have deliberately trapped their victims into doing something for which they could be charged. In one story, a Spanish Inquisitor approaches a maker of holy images and offers to buy one of his statues at a fraction of its usual cost. Unaware of his customer's identity, the sculptor swears that such an offer is an insult to his craftsmanship and that he would rather smash his work than sell it so dear. Goaded beyond endurance by the mockery of the Inquisitor, the poor fellow makes good his word and is immediately arrested as a desecrator of sacred images. Foxe tells us that he was later burned[27] and, to eliminate any lingering doubts that might perplex his readers, concludes:

The abuse of this inquisition is most execrable. If any word shall pass out of the mouth of any, which may be taken in evil part, yea, though no word be spoken, yet if they bear any grudge or evil will against the party, incontinent they command him to be taken, and put into a horrible prison, and then find out crimes against him at their leisure, and in the meantime, no man living is so hardy as once to open his mouth for him.[28]

As William Warner paraphrased it, "This Spanish Inquisition is a Trap so slyly set, / As into it Wise, Godly, Rich, by Blanchers base are set."[29]

Once the trap was sprung, what legal process, if any, was used against the victim? The Protestant writers were unanimous in their opinion and severe in their judgment. Montanus was correct in stating that once a denunciation was received the intended victim was carefully watched to obtain new evidence, and if none was forthcoming he would usually be arrested and adjured to confess his faults.[30] No accusation was made, the names of witnesses were suppressed, and his advocate was leagued with the prosecution against him.[31] All things had to be done "hugger mugger and in close corners, by ambiages, by covert ways and secret counsels," while the prisoner was forbidden to communicate with the outside world.[32] As the theoretical purpose of all this was not justice but the salvation of souls, the whole process could be dragged out for years in the hope of obtaining a confession and unfeigned repentance.[33]

The only real inaccuracy in this account of Inquisitorial procedure lay in the assumption that anyone's testimony was accepted, be they malicious or insane, so long as it was damaging to the prisoner.[34] In reality, the accused could secure his release by proving that the witnesses against him were malicious. To do this it was customary for the prisoner to submit a list of those whom he suspected of bearing him a grudge. If the name of a witness appeared on the list, that man's testimony was immediately discounted by the examiners.[35] Moreover, the Inquisitors often ignored dubious testimony at their own discretion. Montanus himself admits this when he tells of a "frantic" woman who revealed the existence of the "Lutheran" community in Seville. She had been at one time a member of the group but had gone mad and was imprisoned in the attic of one of these "godly" men. Escaping, she told all to the Inquisitors who, "forgetting themselves and their own practices," ignored her and sent her back, to the great relief of some very real heretics.[36]

During the lengthy process of investigation, the defendant was lodged in the prisons of the Inquisition rather than in a secular jail. His plight afforded our writers a superb opportunity for embroidery. Foxe dramatically located him "in a place where he cannot see so much as the ground where he is, and is not suffered either to read or to write, but there endureth in darkness palpable, in horrors infinite, in fear miserable, wrestling with the assaults of death."[37] Montanus, too, claimed that the prisoners were treated worse than dogs. They were imprisoned together, several at a time, in holes which he compared to "Little Ease,"[38] thus contradicting his earlier claim that they were deprived of all human contact.

Actually, the whole picture of Inquisitorial prisons as it was presented to the English was quite wide of the mark. Foxe and Montanus imply that they were more frightful and noisome than most, but such evidence as we possess seems to point in the other direction. Professor Lea discovered, for example, that prisoners frequently sought transfer to them to escape the even greater discomfort of the secular jails.[39] While this may point only to the deplorable state of all Spanish prisons, it is hard to see how they could have been much worse than those of Elizabethan England. We also know, from the fact that Luis de León composed his *De los Nombres de Cristo* while in their care, that the Inquisitors did not invariably deprive their guests of writing materials. The inescapable conclusion is that Foxe and his Spanish contemporary were guilty of distortion and exaggeration.

This invidious tampering with the facts reached serious proportions when they came to deal with the more sensational subject of torture. The Inquisition, like many other courts of the day, employed this "brutish and beastly madness"[40] to extract confessions and testimony from recalcitrant witnesses. Common as this practice was throughout Europe, Foxe made it seem as though the Spanish variety were exceptional in its savagery:

Add moreover to the distresses and horrors of the prison, the injuries, threats, whippings and scourgings, irons, tortures and racks which they there endure. Sometimes also they are brought out, and showed forth to the people as a symbol of rebuke and infamy. And thus they are detained there, some many years, and murdered by long torments, and whole days together are treated more cruelly out of all comparison, than if they were in the hangman's hands to be slain all at once.[41]

The importance of such charges is obvious to anyone who has been exposed to the Black Legend. The Spanish, or the Chinese, have traditionally been credited with devising almost every rare and exotic torture known to man, though the Germans have now somewhat supplanted both. Grisly though the subject may be, it is therefore necessary to examine it in several connections, the first of which is the tortures themselves. Lea's statement is perhaps the most explicit:

... the popular impression that the inquisitorial torture chamber was the scene of an exceptional refinement in cruelty, of specially ingenious modes of inflicting agony, and of a peculiar persistance in extorting confessions, is an error due to sensational writers who have exploited credulity. The system was evil in conception and execution, but the Spanish Inquisition, at least, was not responsible for its introduction, and, as a rule, was less cruel than the secular courts in its applications, and confined itself more strictly to a few well-known methods.[42]

These were generally of two basic varieties: the water torture, in which jars of water were poured down the victim's throat, or the rack, which was used in several ways. More often, the subject was simply threatened with torture in the presence of the implements and commanded to confess.[43] Once administered, torture could not be repeated, and its duration was limited to one hour, though over-enthusiastic officials sometimes extended this to as much as three.[44] Not only Foxe, but Montanus and the pamphleteers were oblivious of these restrictions. Montanus in particular was convinced that the torture could be prolonged indefinitely, and went so far as to invent the use of hot coals,[45] one of the torments expressly prohibited by the Instructions of Valencia in 1561.[46] In all of these writers, the descriptions of the tortures were sensational and minutely detailed, with Montanus reaching depths worthy of the Marquis de Sade.[47] His translator, Thomas Skinner, neatly summarized the whole matter:

... the monstrous racking of men without order of law, the villainous tormenting of naked women beyond all humanity, their miserable death without pity or mercy, the most reproachful triumphing of the Popish Synagogoge over Christians as over Paynims and Ethnics ... ought surely.... to move us to compassion.[48]

The final end of the victims was even more worthy of a passing sigh. Like the mechanics of torture, the *auto de fe* was a highly regulated, even ritualized, affair. Its public nature ensured that the penalties had to be uniform, and the Suprema, or governing council, notoriously frowned on innovations. While the possible sentences ranged from a simple recantation of error to burning alive, the procedure in each case was rigidly controlled by custom and official edict. Thus, floggings were limited to either one hundred or two hundred strokes, and burning was to be preceded by quick strangulation, except in those rare cases where a heretic was judged both sane and unrepentant. Corporal punishment could take no other form than flogging or burning, and, in such cases, secular officials were called upon to supply the violence. As Montanus remarked, if this were penance, it varied considerably from that sacrament as used by the primitive Church;[49] but it hardly compared to the red-hot pincers and boiling lead used on William of Orange's assassin or the Anabaptists of Münster. As with torture, the cruelty of the *auto de fe* was great but not exceptional by the standards of the day.

Seen through the eyes of our writers this picture is greatly altered. If Richard Hasleton, who was seized in Majorca after escaping from a Turkish galley, had received five hundred lashes as he says,[50] he would not have survived to write a pamphlet about it. There is also no evidence to support the claim that Hawkins's men received up to three hundred lashes apiece at an *auto de fe* in Mexico.[51] Two hundred is the maximum recorded limit, and any more would probably have proved fatal to men weakened by long imprisonment.

John Foxe was either more imaginative or less discriminating in his choice of anecdotes, for even when the Spanish were not responsible for the mistreatment of a Protestant, he somehow managed to implicate them in such a way as to exaggerate their brutality. On one such occasion, an English merchant residing in Portugal is said to have satisfied his enmity toward Rome by seizing the consecrated host in the presence of a cardinal and the Portuguese King, throwing it down and stamping on it. After some deliberation, the Portuguese repeatedly drew a knotted linen cloth through his esophagus, cut off his hands, and roasted him over a slow fire; all of which, says Foxe, was done "after the fashion of Spain."[52] Now Foxe, though he put the worst possible construction on such things, was a relatively honest man, and it is quite possible that such an event took place. There is, however, no evidence to suggest that Portugal learned savagery from Spain. In fact, the usual Spanish penalty for sacrilegious outrage was abjuration, appearance at an *auto*, and one hundred lashes. If anything, the Englishman's fate recalls that of a young French noble who was convicted at Abbeville of desecrating a wooden cross. This unfortunate, after a farcical trial, suffered the amputation of his tongue and right hand, following which he was burned alive.[53]

From this brief, and admittedly incomplete summary, it should be evident that English readers were being subjected to propaganda in the modern sense: a conscious and systematic attempt to control their attitudes in the interests of Protestantism. This attempt relied on the exaggeration of actual circumstances while avoiding obvious lies, and implied that the activities described were unique, when in fact they were nothing of the kind. The English government not only condoned the use of torture but actively and publicly defended it in spite of its being generally forbidden by common law.[54] In one of the most remarkable documents ever prepared by high officialdom, Lord Burghley[55] justified the torture of Catholics on grounds familiar to any inquisitor: they deserved it for refusing to give evidence against themselves.[56] Praiseworthy though this severity may have been, it was tempered by Christian charity. In the interests of justice, torture was reserved only for those presumed guilty[57]—a provision that must have been of little comfort to the priests, who realized that the presumption of guilt was all but universal. Very few of them escaped excruciating torments on the way to the scaffold; yet the government, with consummate hypocrisy, could claim that their treatment was not cruel.[58] After all, as the pamphlet says, Edmund Campion was never so thoroughly racked that he was unable to write a confession or sign his name to it![59]

In fairness to Montanus, it should be noted that these horrors occurred after the probable date of his death, but Foxe and the men who were adding fresh embroidery to the *Acts and Monuments* until well into the nineteenth century cannot plead this excuse. Fear calls forth all sorts of injustice, and both nations, in the sixteenth and seventeenth centuries, were deeply afraid. Spain genuinely regarded heretics and Protestants as a menace, while the English were terrified by the threat of Catholic conspiracies. If either nation could claim a moral advantage in its atrocious treatment of suspected enemies, it was Spain, where torture was at least regulated and could be administered only under official surveillance. The victim was thus protected from some of the more fiendish tortures and from the tender mercies of such monsters as Roger Topcliffe, who was encouraged to extract confessions in the privacy of his home with the connivance of the authorities.[60] Many a man left the chambers of the Inquisition broken in body and spirit, but he had the meager comfort of knowing that his sufferings had been prescribed and recorded in ludicrous detail under a recognized system of law. The victims of Roger Topcliffe, in the short time that remained to them, could only reflect that they had been handed over by the government for the private amusement of a sadist.

The reasons for this manifest outrage were obvious. The Marian persecutions had accomplished little save the alienation of public opinion, and the counselors of Elizabeth sought to avoid a similar mistake. Their use of Topcliffe to avoid responsibility is reminiscent of the Inquisitor's device by which prisoners were "relaxed" to the secular authorities for punishment. Though rather transparent, these expedients must have salved the harder consciences in both countries while rendering an already appalling situation worse, particularly with regard to the ultimate disposal of unrepentant victims. The burnings that so horrified Foxe and his compatriots were generally preceded by quick strangulation, but even where they were not, they were merciful compared to the English practice. Anxious as they were to avoid the sigma of persecutor, the English authorities maintained that their Catholic victims were being punished for treason, not heresy. The fact that many of these men were loyal Englishmen in no way pacified those to whom Catholicism and treason were synonymous. It was as traitors that the priests and Jesuits were hanged, drawn, and quartered, and as such, their fate was far more horrible than anything meted out at an *auto de fe*.

Invidious comparisons of this kind are not intended to absolve Spain or foster Anglophobia, but only to put our writers in their proper context. Had they been aware of the anti-Catholic persecutions, Foxe and Montanus would no doubt have felt that as papists and servants of the Antichrist, the English Catholics got what they deserved. Temperamentally, there was nothing so like a devout

Spanish Catholic as an equally devout Protestant reformer, and while, like Foxe, they may have been kind men personally, they rarely pretended to be humanitarians on general grounds. The purpose of these writers was to record the sufferings of those whom they regarded as the only true martyrs: the Protestants, Lollards, and Hussites. In so doing, they slandered both Spain and Catholicism, but Spain fared the worst, for even among Catholics, it remains, indelibly, the land of those "holy Fathers of the Inquisition, the cattercap devils, Doctors (I should say) that like bloody butchers continually thirst after blood."[61]

Ever thereafter, crises in Anglo-Spanish relations were met with renewed English interest in the Inquisition. The pamphleteers of 1588 saw Inquisitors, armed with suitable instruments of torture, aboard every Spanish ship, while Buckingham's Cádiz expedition was followed in 1630 by James Wadsworth's *The English-Spanish Pilgrime or, a New Discoverie of Spanish Popery and Iesuitical Stratagems*. In the midst of Cromwell's comic-opera designs on the West Indies, Samuel Clark discovered that in 1588 the Inquisitors had intended to flog every English citizen over the age of seven to death and to brand the remainder with an "L" for Lutheran, reserving them for perpetual slavery.[62]

These are, of course, but a few of the examples available. Taken together with Foxe and Montanus as a cornerstone, they represent a formidable edifice of exaggeration whose effectiveness lies in its utter credibility. Their assertions, upon which others have built so well, frequently approach the truth; but by a clever use of dramatization and hyperbole they contrived a picture of the Inquisition that is wholly misleading. Its importance to the overall English view of the nation that invented and condoned such a monstrosity cannot be minimized.

CHAPTER IV. THE REVOLT OF THE NETHERLANDS

In the preceding chapters we have dealt with what might be called the preconditions of English anti-Hispanism. They have included the incipient xenophobia of an island race becoming conscious of its nationhood, and religious antagonism, fortified by the vigorous self-criticism of the Spaniards themselves. It is now necessary to look at a more immediate cause of anti-Spanish feeling: the revolt of the Netherlands.

This long and terrible struggle for independence, virtually un-paralleled until modern times, had an enormous effect on English public opinion. Even today, many regard it as one of the great watersheds of human history, a primal confrontation between all that is good, true, and liberal and the powers of darkness, intolerance, and superstition. That such a view is incredibly naive goes without saying; that it presupposes a system of values not universally ac-cepted even by those who believe its legends is irrelevant. It has become a commonplace of popular belief and was, until quite recent-ly, acceptable to many scholars as well. Spain, as the power of dark-ness in question, has obviously suffered from this interpretation, but so has European historiography. Traditionally, the excesses of the "liberal" Protestant school have been laid at the door of such nineteenth-century historians as Motley and Bakhuizen van den Brink, but their works merely reflect the sixteenth-century sources that came most readily to their hands. These were, of course, the memoirs, chronicles, and pamphlets composed by contemporary Dutch and English writers. That these chronicles were available to Elizabethan readers while their equally impressive Spanish coun-terparts were not goes a long way toward explaining the origins of the Black Legend.

The interest aroused in England by the revolt was in itself ex-traordinary. On the surface, at least, it had little to do with English problems, and, as a revolt against an anointed king, it should not have appealed to the imagination of a self-consciously monarchical society. That it did so is to the credit of a group of men whose activities during this period have always intrigued historians. It is perhaps misleading to speak of a Puritan party in Elizabethan England, for the links between men of similar views were far more tenuous than they would be today. Nevertheless, something of the kind did exist with such figures as Walsingham, Leicester, and Sir Philip Sidney as its leading spokesmen in high places. From these great men, long tentacles of power and patronage reached down through the great merchants of the City and the knights in Parliament to humble preachers and pamphleteers. The strength and immutability of these ties should not be exaggerated. The age of manifestos and party cells had not yet begun, and political connections were often those of prudence or quasi-feudal attachment. But for all the absence of party registrations, one thing remains certain: there were those in England who leaned toward the doctrines of John Calvin, who felt a kinship with their coreligionists in the Netherlands, and who were willing and able to make their voices heard. It was these men, or those supported by their patronage, who wrote the history of the Dutch revolt. One may use the dedications of works on this subject as a catalog of those who opposed Spanish designs in Council or in Parliament, and who sought in one way or another to bring the Church of England closer to the Genevan ideal. Sir Francis Walsingham and the Earl of Leicester are perhaps the most prominent, both in real power and in the number of dedications addressed to them, and while their exact theological views may remain a matter for conjecture, their sympathies in this case were clear.

Much the same can be said on the Dutch side. Many of the works which found their way to the English booksellers were translations of Dutch and French originals. For the most part, they too seem to be the work of Calvinists. Though these stern sectarians may not be wholly responsible for Dutch independence, they were unquestionably the most extreme and vocal of its protagonists. Above all, they were inclined to see the revolt in moral terms, and they communicated that view in their writings. When William the Silent, with his remarkable talent for noisy invective, entered the lists on their side, Spain was assured of the worst possible treatment the printed page could afford.

Naturally, Spain was forced to bear the entire burden of responsibility for the carnage that engulfed the Netherlands between

1565 and 1608. As we have seen, the Dutch and English writers chose to regard the Inquisition as a major source of trouble, but other reasons were advanced from time to time. Jacobus Verheiden, writing at the end of this weary epoch, professed to see no other cause than "the exceeding spacious and bottomless gulf of the Spanish ambition and hate which they bare unto our Nation, which so totally possessed the mind of Philip and all Spaniards."[1] The great Welsh soldier, Sir Roger Williams, discovered more subtle but equally unflattering reasons:

> The state of Spain, as I said in my discourse of their discipline, is governed by two sorts of people, captains and clergy. The captains animate the king to wars, to maintain their wealth and greatness; so doth the clergy to maintain their estate against those of the religion [the Protestants]. By these means, the ambition of the Duke D'Alva, of Cardinal Granvelle, and their seconds, persuaded the king to undertake to subdue the Netherlanders at his pleasure; to lay upon them such gabels, taxes, and all manner of tributes as should please the king to demand.[2]

Williams's judgment may have been based on his soldierly distrust of politicians, for in general he respected the Spaniards; but whatever else may be said of his statement, it certainly identified the true leaders of the "war party" at Philip's court.

It is now obvious that these charges must have been profoundly shocking to the king, who had envisioned no more than a logical system of government that would simplify administration and balk the disruptive powers of the great noblemen. As far as religious persecution was concerned, he was merely carrying out the program begun by his father, a native of the Netherlands. He failed to realize, as so many reformers are apt to do, that his innovations entailed a complete change in many people's lives and were, in any event, wholly divorced from political reality. His subjects, noted for their financial acumen, quickly realized that the end result of all this would be higher taxation and, for the nobility, an almost complete loss of privilege.[3] Perhaps the most balanced contemporary assessment of the affair appeared in an anonymous history of Antwerp, published in 1586:

. . . neither religion on one side, nor the chastisement of rebellion on the other side, was all that was aimed at or sought for of either, but popular factions and inordinate liberty (a pestilent poison to all kingdoms and dominions most to be feared in these our days) crept in & was nourished in the midst of many the subjects, and in the Prince's heart there was a most fervent desire inflamed to reduce that province to a kingdom.[4]

Such sophistication was extremely rare. For several centuries to come, all blame was successfully shifted to the bloodthirsty Spaniards and their king. Later apologists, like Verheiden, found this congenial as it enabled them to argue that Philip possessed all the attributes of a tyrant and was therefore no longer entitled to obedience.[5] In the beginning, though, a more traditional argument prevailed. As the king's position in a rigidly hierarchical society was unassailable, William of Orange, the first and greatest of the rebel apologists, declared that their quarrel was really with the venal counselors who had misled the king.[6] Chief among them was the notorious Duke of Alba.

Sending Alba to the Netherlands was probably a serious mistake. This stern, unbending nobleman, the greatest soldier of his generation, looked upon the Netherlanders as mere rebels and upon their country as a province to be conquered and ruled. With the help of a superb army of veterans, he was able to translate his thoughts into action with such efficiency that he made his name a byword for severity and provided generations of pamphleteers and historians with ample cause for indignation. Reconciliation between Philip and his Netherlandish subjects became all but impossible, and the popular accounts of Alba's behavior became a major ingredient in the Black Legend.

According to Thomas Churchyard, the English soldier and literary hack, Alba accomplished by cruelty what others would have done by "sweet persuasion."[7] When he arrived in the summer of 1567, the situation may not have been irretrievable. Many of the greatest nobles, including Orange, were still following a middle course: demanding a restoration of their ancient privileges but holding fast in their allegiance to the Crown. The rebellion launched by the more radical group under Brederode had been summarily crushed, largely through the efforts of the Netherlanders themselves, and the way was open to an attempt at conciliation.[8] Unfortunately, neither Alba nor his master intended anything of the kind. Determined at all costs to assert royal authority over the rebellious magnates, Alba immediately created a special court, the purpose of which was to punish those guilty of participation in the recent disorders. This Council of Troubles, popularly known as the Council of Blood, was said to have slain between eighteen and twenty thousand people,[9] and the farther removed the writers were from events, the more spectacular did its cruelties become. By the middle of the seventeenth century it was reported that

they have killed women great with child, and ripped up their bellies, and taken out the child and killed it; and some they have flayed alive, and covered drums heads with their skins; and some they have tied to a post, and made a small fire round about them, and so roasted them to death.[10]

At the same time, several stories that had evidently attracted no attention at the time appeared. In one we are told that the Council beheaded a widow at Utrecht for giving a Protestant preacher lodging for the night. In another, a man was hanged for sheltering his own son from the persecutors.[11] As the contemporary historian of Antwerp put it: "Thus having glutted himself with the blood of this people, and through his extreme cruelties wrought a dreadful terror of himself in their hearts, he then published again the inquisition, and they durst not but obey."[12]

It is a remarkable record, the more so because this same author claimed that the Council had executed 1,700 citizens in Antwerp alone.[13] The depredations of Alba and his colleagues were unquestionably great, but these figures must have been a deliberate exaggeration, for research has shown that of the 12,302 people condemned by the tribunal, only 1,105 were executed or banished.[14] Equally dubious was the charge that a list of "articles or conditions" found in the chambers of a Council member demanded the destruction of sacred images, that the Protestants might be accused of sacrilege, and the impoverishment of the country, that it might be easier to control.[15]

The initial effects of this reign of terror were quite satisfactory from the Spanish point of view. Military resistance under the leadership of William of Orange collapsed through lack of popular support,[16] and for a time the rebellion languished. It was not until 1572, five years after his first appearance in the Low Countries, that Alba was once again forced to march against armed insurgents. His attempt to impose a sales tax of 10 percent had done what his restrictions on political and religious liberty had failed to do, and the important provinces of Holland and Zeeland were openly declaring for the Prince of Orange. The campaign that followed provided the opponents of Alba with yet more ammunition for propaganda.

From the start, Alba seems to have pursued a variant of the policy of terrorism that had worked so well before. The account of his doings as they appeared in a digested chronicle of 1598 make grim reading:

> The second of October Mechlin was forcibly taken and spoiled, wherein many Burghers were murdered, & many women and maids deflowered.
>
> The Spaniards took Zutphen where they used the Burghers very cruelly.
>
> Don Frederick [Alba's son] entered into Naarden, where contrary to his faith and promise he murdered divers Burghers and burnt the town.[17]

This terse recitation of horrors is dramatic enough for the modern reader, but his sixteenth-century forebear demanded more, and was not to be disappointed. The examples of embroidery on this theme of sacking towns are too numerous to be cataloged, and one extract, dealing with the destruction of Naarden, will have to suffice.

According to the *Tragicall History*, the Spanish troops were "lovingly received" by the citizens and peacefully billeted themselves without further ado. That evening, at Don Frederick's order, the people were told to assemble at the hospital chapel to receive the new ordinances proclaimed by his father. "But when the miserable citizens were come thither, the Spaniards murdered every mother's son of them, sacked and burnt the town, ravished the women, yea, and murdered some of them, and left the rest live in great martyrdom."[18] In the midst of the carnage, a young lad escaped and sought refuge in a nearby wood. As he wept bitter tears, a youth in shining white appeared, comforted him, cursed the Spaniards, and vanished as mysteriously as he had come. The child's father, it seems, had been killed, and "his mother being ravished, was hanged by the arms of the tyrannous Spaniards, and when the fire came and took hold of her house, she being tied by the arms, could not get away, so that she was burnt in her own house."[19]

Such tales have a high imaginative content, but they should not be discounted altogether. The long and desperate siege of Haarlem proved that there was indeed a policy of deliberate atrocity and that, for once, the policy failed. Terrified by reports reaching them from the South, the burghers refused to open their city gates; and after disease, starvation, and bitter assaults forced them to surrender, Don Frederick admitted the error of his ways by sparing them further misery.[20] Haarlem was thus a turning point, and before long Alba himself returned to Spain, leaving the more gentle Requesens in his place.

He also left a legacy of hatred that has not been forgotten. To the humanitarian his policies were indefensible, and to the unthinking his conduct has been regarded as typical of the cruel and haughty Castilian. Though Williams thought Philip a fool to replace him,[21] Alba's complete inability to appreciate the Netherlanders' point of view made him unsuited to the direction of their affairs. His rule in the Netherlands was a dismal climax to a long and distinguished career and brought down lasting infamy not only upon himself but upon those who carried out his orders.

This is hardly the place to undertake his defense, but much could be said against the proposition that Spain as a whole shares in whatever guilt may have been his. Let us but note in passing that his army in 1573 contained only 7,900 Spaniards out of a total complement of 54,300. Of the remainder, by far the largest number (30,400) were natives of the Netherlands who were presumably willing to carry out the Duke's orders.[22] Thus it is hard to believe that the sole responsibility for the horrors at Mechlin and Naarden lies with the small minority of Spaniards involved. Not only Netherlandish troops but Netherlandish captains must share the blame for these atrocities. It was the Walloon nobleman, Berleimont, who inundated the Waterlant and put its inhabitants to the sword, and it was his compatriot Bossu who sacked Rotterdam—a fact that Williams alone among the Dutch and English writers appears to have remembered.[23] On the rebel's side, it should be remembered that Lumey de la Marck, leader of the Sea Beggars, personally tortured and executed priests, while his followers committed such outrages that many towns feared to admit them.[24] These facts, of course, were long in reaching England, and even today it is not fully appreciated that the revolt of the Netherlands was at times very like a civil war. As with the conquest of the New World, no one should be called upon to excuse what the Spaniards did, but neither should their deeds be regarded as unique and unparalleled examples of barbarity.

Unfortunately, the removal of Alba failed to have the desired effect. Spain's good will, and indeed its reputation, was placed once again in the balance by the sack of Antwerp. The story of this wholly unintended tragedy has its origins in the financial difficulties of Philip II. Not even the riches of Potosí seemed capable of financing the manifold projects of the "Prudent King," and his soldiers were, more often than not, unpaid and underfed for intolerably long periods of time. This sort of treatment, however unintentional, breeds sedition even among the most disciplined of troops; and in 1576, an unfortunate conjunction of affairs called forth a mutiny which, as Geyl said, ensured the ultimate failure of Spanish designs in Holland and Zeeland.[25] In the previous autumn, Philip had declared the Spanish treasury bankrupt and left his troops to face a Northern winter with their pay twenty-two months in arrears. With the untimely death of Requesens on March 5, 1576, the troops found themselves leaderless as well as penniless, and as no successor had been appointed, they elected a leader of their own. Abandoning the siege of Zierekzee, they moved off to seek food and remuneration by sacking Antwerp as they had threatened to do two years before.[26] Further aggravated by the attempt of the states to raise an army against them, the mutinous *tercios* fell upon the hapless city and subjected its population to all the horrors of rape, murder, and pillage. In all, seven thousand townspeople are said to have lost their lives.[27]

The most circumstantial account of the tragedy was written by George Gascoigne, the poet, soldier of fortune, and sometime member of Parliament who was himself present at the time. Though he arbitrarily raised the number of fatal casualties to seventeen thousand,[28] we are not to suppose that this is a malicious exaggeration. Aware that his reporting would seem highly colored to an impartial reader, he tells us, "if I were disposed to write maliciously about the vanquishers, their former barbarous cruelty, insolence, rapes, spoils, incests, and sacrileges committed in sundry other places, might yield sufficient matter without the lawful remembrance of this their late stratagem."[29] If the cynic lifts an eyebrow at such objectivity, it is only fair to note that Gascoigne was willing to praise the valor and discipline of the Spanish and point by way of contrast to the pusillanimity of the Walloons who defended the city.[30] It is unfortunate that, in this instance at least, a contribution to the Black Legend seems to reflect a large measure of historical truth. For once, the attacking forces were composed almost entirely of Spaniards, and their crimes were committed, not in the heat of battle, but "when the blood was cold and they now victors without resistance."[31] It is probable that, as another writer said, even the Catholic religious houses were forced to disgorge their coin and plate,[32] and that "the *Rich* was spoiled because he had; and the *Poor* were hanged because they had nothing."[33]

Though such behavior was far from uncommon in sixteenth-century warfare, the fall of Antwerp caught and held the English imagination as no other foreign disaster was able to do. Preachers compared it to the Fall of Jerusalem. Moralists saw it as a divine chastisement, a warning to the sinful Londoners to mend their ways and eschew the luxury that had weakened Antwerp's moral fiber and brought about its collapse.[34] It was also, of course, an ideal vehicle for something not unlike pornography. By Cromwell's day, anti-Spanish pamphleteers were describing the most horrid and obscene torments imaginable with vivid relish.[35] So great was the demand for this entertainment that Gascoigne's pamphlet was produced as a stage play.

A Larum for London or the Siedge of Antwerpe should serve to remind us that not all Elizabethan playwrights were touched with genius. It is basically a crude one-act play into which the anonymous author strove to compress as much bloodshed and rapine as possible.

If it contains a moral, it is that citizens should always be militarily prepared and should be generous to disabled soldiers. The villain of the piece is one "Sancto Danila," presumably the Spanish commander Sancho D'Avila, but all of the Spanish captains in the Netherlands are made to share responsibility for the sack. They had, it seems, been conspiring for years to seize the wealth of Antwerp, and even Alba is pictured as returning from Spain for the occasion. The action itself is little more than a series of uncoordinated murders, chases, and rapes, but there is a deliberate attempt to arouse patriotic sentiment in the audience. The factor of an English merchant house is forced to prostrate himself before the unconscionable Alba and is finally treated to the strappado in an attempt to relieve him of his money. No sooner is he released than "Danila" appears and tortures him again for the same purpose. In the meantime, chaos reigns on stage as the hero, a one-legged Flemish war veteran, intervenes from time to time to rescue some highborn dame from mass rape.[36]

Nonsense this may be, but it would be folly to deny its effectiveness. The events that inspired the play were bad enough without elaboration, and judging by the interest they aroused in later writers, the sack of Antwerp must be regarded as an important part of the Elizabethan Black Legend. Fortunately, it was also one of the last such ingredients to come out of the Low Countries. Requesen's successors managed, for the most part, to avoid further atrocities in the interests of policy. It is a good thing that they did so, for each of the inevitable minor lapses was carefully noted by the pamphleteers.[37]

Important as these individual incidents may have been, their effect could scarcely have been greater than the shock produced throughout the Protestant world by the murder of the Prince of Orange. As the chief leader of the Netherlands revolt and its greatest spokesman, William had written a series of violent and frequently scandalous proclamations and treatises, the most famous of which was his *Apology*.[38] In addition to this major work of villification, he had produced or inspired a number of less ambitious efforts. His *Supplication to the Kings Maiesty of Spayne* may be taken as an example. Published in England in 1573, it maintained the hoary fiction that his revolt was directed not against Philip but against the Duke of Alba and pleaded for the latter's removal as a menace to the King's best interests. This praiseworthy consideration for the King did not prevent William from speaking his mind about the Spanish officials, whose "envy and cancred malice, being further incensed and stuffed with insatiable avarice and unmeasurable prodigialities,"[39] had laid waste the entire country. Thus echoing the charges he had made in his first *Declaration and Publication* of 1568, he moved on to new and lower ground with an attack on the morals of the Spanish soldiery. Like all good propagandists, he was well aware that no picture is quite so successful in stirring up popular rage as that of wives and daughters being subjected to unnatural assaults by a brutal and licentious soldiery. Accordingly, we find "honest women and young maidens" raped before their husbands and fathers, while pregnant women are butchered in the streets by men who had given themselves over to all kinds of unnatural vice.[40]

William told this sort of thing almost too well; but whether in spite of such gifts, or partially because of them, he was thought of in England as the holy and guiding spirit of the Dutch resistance. Now he was dead, murdered by a hireling of Spain in the courtyard of his own palace. It must have seemed a terrible disaster to the cause, but oddly enough, when the news was brought to England, an unparalleled opportunity for invective was lost. The author of the pamphlet that reported the deed, though obviously a friend to the slain leader, said only that the killer, when questioned, confessed that he had committed the crime "at the Prince of Parma's request, and other Princes, at whose hands he should receive for doing the same, 25,000 crowns."[41] He did not refer to the well-known fact that Philip himself had set a price on the Prince's head, nor did he resort to the biblical denunciation that was to color Emanuel van Meteren's retrospective account of the deed. With only a simple statement of circumstances, the author hurried on to a more congenial task: a lengthy description of the barbarous tortures to which the assassin was subjected during his four-day execution. On the surface, it might appear that this effort represents a contribution to some anti-Dutch Black Legend, but this is not the case. William the Silent was a man of great popularity in the England of his day, and has since become something of a folk hero on both sides of the Channel. A simple statement of his martyrdom was sufficient to seal

Spain's guilt in the eyes of many, and the gruesome details of the Dutch revenge would not have seemed so reprehensible to an age accustomed to public executions and the use of torture. Rhetoric would have been superfluous.

The assassination of William was the first of a series of events which caused England to reexamine its position with regard to the Low Countries. On August 7, 1585, Antwerp, for all its vicissitudes the wealthiest city in the Netherlands, fell once again to the skill of the Spaniards and the dissensions of its inhabitants. Holland and Zeeland were left dangerously exposed.[42] Aware of the importance of the Netherlands as a Spanish citadel in the North and alarmed at Spain's callous disregard of commercial interests in England's greatest market, Elizabeth had long been sending volunteers and financial aid across the Narrow Seas.[43] Now more direct intervention was called for. In early October the first English troops arrived, to be followed in December by the Earl of Leicester. As the troops embarked, Elizabeth, ever mindful of public opinion, published *A Declaration of the Causes Moving the Queen of England to give aid to the Defence of the People afflicted and oppressed in the Lowe Countries.* Unlike most contributions to anti-Hispanism, this is a piece of official propaganda, and as such, indicates that the Crown was not unduly disturbed by the anti-Spanish enthusiasms of independent pamphleteers. Maintaining, as did Orange, that the King could do no wrong, Elizabeth complained that Philip's counsellors had led him to appoint "men more exercised in wars than in peaceable government, and some of them notably delighted in blood as hath appeared by their actions, to be the chiefest governors of all his said Low Countries, contrary to the ancient laws and customs thereof."[44] Thus the Crown itself, not yet divested of its mystical qualities, gave official sanction to English anti-Hispanism without hedge or cavil. Spanish counselors were declared guilty of sending bloodthirsty Spanish tyrants to the Netherlands, under whose rule a brutal Spanish soldiery was permitted to ravage the peaceful countryside.[45] Spread abroad not only in pamphlet form but in the august pages of Holinshed, Camden, and Baker, the *Declaration* gave Englishmen the Queen's word for what they had long suspected.

There is no telling where this new incentive to pamphleteering might have led had not the Armada intervened to steal public interest away from the Dutch. The hacks and pamphleteers turned their attention to more pressing concerns, and it was left to respectable historians to complete their work.

The chronicles of Holinshed, Camden, and Baker, are in many respects better indicators of anti-Spanish feeling than are the pamphlets and outpurings of the Dutch; for they tell, if nothing else, how much was acceptable to a fairly critical intelligence and how much was passed on to future generations. Unlike pamphlets and broadsheets, such expensive and ponderous texts would rarely have been used for fire-lighter. Camden is perhaps the most reliable of the lot, though he was not necessarily the most popular. Holinshed is, of course, famous through its association with Shakespeare, while Baker is said to have been the favorite reading of such as Sir Roger de Coverley.[46] Together, they are a compendium of the historical information available to Englishmen until well into the eighteenth century, and their hostility toward Spain is significant.

Holinshed accused the Spaniards of basely murdering the Prince of Orange, oppressing the Netherlanders, and plotting "subtly and continually" against Elizabeth herself.[47] Like the others, he reprinted the full text of the Queen's *Declaration* and added to it the address of the deputies who had come to ask for aid. Baker reported that "the Duke of Alba, breathing nothing but slaughter and blood, made the Dutch come flocking into England as into a sanctuary"[48] and that under his direction "the Spanish in the Low Countries began to deal roughly with the people and harried the inhabitants with all manner of spoil and injury."[49] Camden refers to "the barbarous cruelty of the Spaniards[50] and, more important, takes his account of the beginnings of the revolt from Emanuel van Meteren.

Meteren deserves separate consideration. His monumental *Historica Belgica* more closely resembled a historical monograph than a chronicle, but regrettably its purpose was alien to both. A native of Antwerp who spent most of his life in London, he took a deep interest in the vicissitudes of his people and was inspired to write a complete narrative of their struggles from his own rigidly Calvinist point of view.[51] Richer in invective than in scholarship, it attracted the attention of Thomas Churchyard, who attempted to translate it into

English as *The Succeeding Governors of the Netherlands.* Though he was, as we have seen, a veteran of the wars and author of a most interesting history under his own name, Churchyard had in this instance to be content with laboring for the glory of another. Characteristically, the task suited him so ill that he not only added sections unthought of by the worthy Meteren but included some of his own experiences as well. Then, in failing health, he turned the bulk of the task over to his friend, the professional translator Richard Robinson. The result is one of the most curious potpourries in historical literature. The fulminations of the good Fleming alternate with the common-sense remarks of the translator and scholarly interjections from John Stow and others to produce an effect not unlike that of a paper written as a cooperative project in a madhouse.

Churchyard, who respected his enemies, began the text with a brief discussion of the causes of the rebellion together with a hilarious account of his own experiences during its earlier stages. He then introduced the next part of his tale by referring to that "great, noble soldier, the Duke of Alba."[52] Within two pages, a section written by Meteren is describing the Duke as "a notable person, no doubt, but a notable cruel tyrant, tall of personage, lean of body, (like unto Brutus or Cassius whom Caesar censured to be feared)."[53] To complete the confusion, we are told that he was the greatest Spanish soldier of his day,[54] who ruled with great cruelty, killing men, women, and children without restraint.[55] Unaccountably, Philip, who is usually described in terms more appropriate to the Antichrist than to a Christian ruler, was sufficiently appalled at this excess to secure the Duke's removal.[56]

For all this addled approach to history—it must have been confusing even to an Elizabethan—there is no doubt as to the purpose of the work. Meteren, at any rate, meant to damn the Spaniards, and his conclusion may be taken as a summary of what all his colleagues were trying to express:

Manifestly thus it appeareth in the sight of God and all the world, what impiety, malice, mischief, and cruelty the Pope and Spanish King hath with foxlike subtlety and lionlike force practiced against the nobles and states of the Low Countries, infringing their ancient privileges, breaking fidelity in contracts, violating the bonds of amity, oppressing all integrity of loyal subjects and faithful servants of God, seeking to make havoc of high and low, rich and poor, young and old, with more than Turkish tyranny in those dominions most intolerable.[57]

Even this does not carry the full flavor of the attack, for his denunciations were often sustained by Holy Writ. The Pope and Spanish King were said to resemble "bloodthirsty Baalac [sic] cursing the Israelites and the other more like Pharaoh persecuting and oppressing them; but both of these most like the raging lion and hungry bear that Solomon speaketh of."[58] The assassins sent against the "chief godly governor, the Prince of Orange," by this "Romish Babylon and Spanish Periander" are called, among other things, "Caitiffs of Cain's crew and Champions of Satan."[59]

Much of this strikes the modern reader as quaintly amusing, but the frequency with which it appears in sixteenth-century writings indicates that many took it seriously. Open denunciation is neither so insidious nor ultimately so successful as the distortion used so cleverly by Las Casas, but it too serves a purpose. Meteren's history, while containing few accounts of specific Spanish atrocities, does provide many a fine mouth-filling oath to fling at the hated enemy; and to some minds, this is a matter of importance. Whatever one's reason for subscribing to a prejudice, it is always enjoyable to hear a prestigious writer concur so heartily.

To conclude in the same vein, there appeared in 1599 a work whose purpose it was to sum up all the characteristics of the Spaniards as revealed by their stay in the Low Countries. Though a trifling piece, abominably ill-written by someone who must at one time have been an innkeeper, it contains most of the mature Black Legend in capsule form, a condensation of what the English reader must have thought had he read deeply in the literature of the revolt. Under sixteen separate headings, the "Signior" is castigated as vain and hypocritical, faithless and cruel. Las Casas's man-eating dogs are recalled along with anecdotes from other sources to prove charges ranging from greed to cowardice. The worst, though, and this is where suspicions of publicanism come to mind, is the "Signior's" behavior when lodged at an inn. We are told that he is "a Devil in his Lodging" because he demands good service and the best beds, "a Wolfe at Table," and "a Hog in his Chamber," filthy in his habits and infected with venereal disease. The author concluded: "How then can the Host in quiet sleep? / Who a Devil, a Wolf, and a Hog doth keep."[60] How indeed!

This, then, was the Spaniard as seen through pro-Dutch eyes; but was there no other picture available to the sixteenth- and seventeenth-century Englishman? Unfortunately, the answer must be no. The examples selected in this chapter are few, but they represent a fair cross-section of those available at the time. Williams and Churchyard, as experienced soldiers, defended Spanish valor,[61] but no one defended Philip, few protested against the crimes of the Beggars, and most tended to exaggerate those of the Spaniards. Of the several histories of the revolt written by Spaniards, not one was circulated in England. Perhaps Philip felt that his case was so obvious that it needed no defense. Certainly by the accepted legal and moral standards of the day this was true, and the atrocities committed in his name were little worse than those usually encountered in sixteenth-century warfare. One is tempted to think, though, that the answer is more obvious. Had there been no agreement of opinion between certain powerful Englishmen and the most vocal element in Dutch politics, the history of the revolt might well have been written differently.

No demonic theory, however, can explain the continuing popularity of the views expressed in this literature. The Netherlanders, whose struggle it was, cannot be blamed for hating their enemies, and their grievances were very real. But could John Lothrop Motley, an American writing three centuries after the event,[62] plead the same excuse? His invective was nearly as picturesque as that of Meteren, and his historical understanding was little more advanced. We must conclude that the rebel's view of Spain retained its appeal because it became associated with a modern system of values. It has been assumed that the Netherlanders were seeking religious tolerance and personal liberty, when in fact many of them sought only to impose another kind of religious tyranny while maintaining aristocratic privilege. The democratic liberties generally associated with their names were, for the most part, unthought of in 1565. Those who, in the nineteenth and early twentieth centuries, believed that these principles were woven into the very fabric of the universe were naturally ignorant of this. They associated the revolt of the Netherlands with the worship of their own gods and made its enemies their enemies. As a result, the part played by Spain in this long and bloody tragedy must take its place among the larger causes of anti-Hispanism, not only in England but throughout all Western Europe.

CHAPTER V. AS UNTO TRAITORS, ROBBERS, AND MURDERERS

England's fledgling attempts at overseas expansion were largely devoid of ideological significance, but in their own way, they too proved a fertile spawning ground of anti-Hispanism. When Elizabeth ascended the throne in 1558, England was already behind in the race for empire. Two generations had passed since Spain and Portugal had divided the non-European world between them, and efforts to increase English prosperity through exploration could now be made only at their expense. Of the two, Spain was, for a number of reasons, the more important rival. The relative proximity and fabled wealth of Spain's American possessions whetted the ambition of Englishmen, while its grandiose territorial claims and steadfast refusal to trade with foreigners frustrated and angered them. It was only natural that attempts would be made to break the Spanish monopoly, and that Spain would oppose these attempts with all its power.

Further contributions to the Black Legend were inevitable. As Spain claimed everything beyond 46°W by virtue of a papal bull and the treaty of Tordesillas, and as its American ports were irrevocably closed to foreign trade, English voyages to this area were clearly illegal. If an English ship should appear without royal commission, it could be presumed that she was engaged either in smuggling or in piracy. If, on the other hand, she sailed with the official knowledge of the Queen, her presence could be regarded only as an act of war. Elizabeth was anxious to avoid open conflict during the first three decades of her reign, and as a result, those Englishmen who visited the Americas did so unofficially, though often with the silent backing of the government. Only the ingenuity of the seamen themselves could thus prevent their seizure and prosecution as pirates by a nation determined at all costs to protect its vast possessions from foreign encroachment. Rigidity in the interpretation of the law was matched by rigidity in its enforcement, and most of the Elizabethan voyages involved at least one unpleasant, and often terminal, encounter with the Spanish authorities. Thanks to the efforts of an unusually literate group of English adventurers, few of these incidents went unreported.

The record of the Elizabethan travelers is unusually complete, and its influence on the developing Black Legend must have been enormous. The English reader could more easily identify with the problems of Drake or Hawkins than with those of foreigners, however sympathetic their cause, and he had ample opportunity to do so through reading the pamphlets which were generally published on the completion of each voyage. The men who wrote them were of varying stature, but all were predictably imbued with anti-Spanish feeling. As eyewitnesses of the scenes they described, their testimony carried great weight, and if the Elizabethan reader was too lazy to search out their individual publications, he could easily find them gathered together in the work of Richard Hakluyt, one of the greatest historians of the sixteenth century.

The influence of this man's work, both on English expansion and on the development of the Black Legend, deserves examination. Though he traveled little himself, his *Principle Voyages, Traffiques and Discoveries of the English Nation* is to many the very symbol of early English expansionism. Crammed with stirring travel accounts, navigational data, and vivid exhortations to carry the Queen's standard to ever more remote corners of the globe, it is an invaluable key to the adventurous Elizabethan spirit and a mine of information on the early voyages. As a result, few such multi-volumed works have enjoyed such popularity. First published in 1589, the entire text was reissued in 1599–1600, 1809–1912, and 1903–1905, while numerous extracts and abridged editions have continued to satisfy the curiosity of more superficial readers.

The author's life may not have been as exciting as the adventures he chronicled, but his unique position in Elizabethan society lends him a degree of interest that transcends the merely picturesque. Richard Hakluyt was a clergyman, diplomat, historian, propagandist, and much else beside, but primarily he was one of the first of a now omnipresent breed—the consulting expert. The rapidly expanding interests of the London merchants made it impossible for them to remain abreast of the latest events and discoveries overseas, and like the businessmen of today they sought the knowledge of a specialist. Hakluyt had been well trained for such a task by an older cousin of the same name. This cousin, though a barrister by profession, found geography more congenial than the law and was able to use the knowledge gleaned in the pursuit of his hobby to supplement his regular income. As adviser to the London merchants, and on at least one occasion to Burghley himself,[1] he was able to launch his more famous kinsman on a career that was to include service to the leading personalities of the day. Michael Locke, Sir Humphrey Gilbert, and Sir Walter Raleigh all profited from the advice of Hakluyt the Younger while Walsingham used him to spy out the colonial ambitions of the French.[2] Lord Howard of Effingham, who commanded the English fleet in Armada Year was his patron, and the Virginia and East India Companies listed him among their founders.[3]

As time went on, public relations gradually superseded these advisory functions. The younger Hakluyt's clients were in need of far more than advice. Specifically, they required both official backing and popular approval if they were to avoid the stigma of piracy. The presence of a scholar and man of letters in their midst could not fail to be used to advantage, and so it was that Hakluyt the learned adviser became Hakluyt the publicist. It was a happy choice, for it gave the world the *Principle Voyages*, but this was only part of his work. Before an assault could be made on public opinion, his carefully mustered arguments had to receive at least the tacit approval of the Queen. The now famous *Discourse concerning Western Planting* was the result. This, the *Principle Voyages*, and a shorter work, the *Divers Voyages Touching the Discouerie of America and the Ilands Adiacent* comprise the bulk of Hakluyt's work and the basis of his claim to fame. Though the audiences to whom they were addressed varied widely, it is worth noting that, as his biographer says, "every appearance of Hakluyt in print was tuned to the same key, the pressing forward of enterprise."[4] But this theme was not without its counterpoint. In interesting the English in colonization, and in publishing their voyages, Hakluyt was unavoidably drawn into stirring up resentment against the chief obstacle to those designs, and that obstacle was not public apathy, but Spain.

Hakluyt's own attitude was fully expressed in the *Discourse concerning Western Planting*, presented to the Queen in 1583. This was, of course, before the Armada, and it is quite possible that the

Queen forbade him to publish it for fear of offending Philip. Whatever the reason, it did not appear for public consumption until 1877
when England had entered upon a new flurry of empire building.
In some ways it is a pity that the Elizabethans were prevented from
seeing it, for while it would undoubtedly have irritated the Spaniards, it is by far the clearest statement of Hakluyt's theories and
prejudices ever to have come from his hand. He begins by noting
that the Spaniards have done great things in the Indies for "filthy
lucre and vain ostentation,"[5] complains of the disruptive influence
of Spanish policy on Europe,[6] and quotes five pages verbatim from
Las Casas in order to prove their depraved and brutal nature.[7] Fortunately for the English, his researches had led him to believe that
Spain's subject nations were restive, and that, owing to a scarcity of
Spanish colonists in many areas, a base in the New World would be
easy to establish.[8] If this were done, great inroads could be made on
Philip's empire, and in Hakluyt's own words, "the Spanish king shall
be left as bare as Aesop's proud crow . . . his pride abated and his
tyranny utterly suppressed."[9] Spanish military power is dismissed
with contempt:

> I may therefore conclude this matter with comparing the Spaniards
> unto a drone, or an empty vessel, which when smitten upon yieldeth a
> great sound and that afar off; but come near and look into them, there is
> nothing in them: or rather like the ass which wrapped himself in a lion's
> skin and marched far off to strike terror into the hearts of the other
> beasts, but when the fox drew near he perceived his long ears and made
> him a jest unto all the beasts of the forest. In like manner, we, (upon peril
> of my life) shall make the Spaniard ridiculous in all Europe, if with pierc-
> ing eyes we see into his contemptible weakness in the West Indies and
> with true style paint him out *ad vivum* unto the world in his faint
> colors.[10]

The canny Elizabeth must have looked with amazement on this
visionary optimism, but even visionaries had their place in her
scheme of things, and while this work never saw print during its
author's lifetime, others like it were not suppressed again. It would
seem, in fact, that Hakluyt's timing had been excellent. Incidents
provoked by his own associates in the New World and the increas-
ingly serious situation in the Netherlands were forcing the Queen to

abandon her policy of peace. As spokesman for a group which tended to favor action on both fronts, Hakluyt was assured of a hearing. He was also assured of a living from the Church which he could scarcely have earned through the exercise of his pastoral duties.

There was only a hint of anti-Hispanism in the *Divers Voyages*,[11] but it emerged once again as a major theme in Hakluyt's magnum opus. As its title indicates, the *Principle Voyages* was no treatise but an extensive compilation of documents and sources relating to the voyages of exploration. Its contributors varied in nationality, character, and purpose—Hakluyt was far too wise to let prejudice interfere with his presentation of useful facts—but his book dealt chiefly with the accomplishments of Englishmen, and it is chiefly from them that he drew his material. In consequence, the *Principle Voyages* presents a view of Spain that, to a remarkable degree, foreshadows the English Black Legend in its final form. Certain qualities and character traits were portrayed as typically Spanish, and with few exceptions, these impressions reflect the hostile nature of the contacts in which they were formed. Foremost among them was the allegation heard even today, that the Spaniards are habitually more cruel and treacherous than other peoples.

Examples of this charge are too numerous to catalog, but one or two deserve retelling. A typical instance, noteworthy both for the indignation with which it was reported and for the doubtful respectability of the English case, is Sir John Hawkins's tale of his defeat at San Juan de Ulúa in 1568. During the preceding year, Hawkins had attempted to sell a cargo of slaves on the Spanish Main in violation of the royal order prohibiting trade between the colonists and foreigners. He had made two similar voyages in the past with some success, but the officials who had then permitted him to land his cargo had in the meantime been reminded of their duty by the imposition of substantial fines. Consequently, they were disinclined to cooperate when Hawkins's small fleet appeared once again in their harbors. At two of the tiny ports he was able to work out an arrangement by which he would appear to capture the place and force its inhabitants to purchase his goods, thereby providing merchandise which was admittedly much in demand while at the same time absolving the local authorities of all blame for having dealings with foreigners. At Rio de la Hacha, however, he ran into genuine opposition from the bellicose treasurer of the community, Miguel de Castellanos, and was forced to seize the town without his connivance and with considerable destruction of property.

It was the Englishman's misfortune, with such credentials, that his flagship was so badly damaged in a storm that he was forced to put into San Juan de Ulúa for repairs. San Juan de Ulúa was the port of Vera Cruz, the gateway to Mexico. Through it passed the wealth of the interior on its way to the mother country, and it was here, as Hawkins well knew, that the *flota* from Spain would anchor in only a matter of days. Only a dire emergency could have led him to risk an encounter with a sizable Spanish fleet, but there was no alternative and his flotilla of seven ships entered the harbor and anchored before the commander of the harbor batteries realized that these were not the visitors he had been expecting. Anxious to proclaim the harmlessness of his intentions, Hawkins quickly gave assurances to the embarassed commander and dispatched messages to Vera Cruz requesting permission to careen his ship and purchase supplies.

The next morning, the English awoke to find thirteen tall ships blocking the entrance to the harbor. As luck would have it, this force was conveying not only the usual cargo of goods for the colonists, but a new viceroy, Don Martín Enriquez, and to Don Martín, the presence of Hawkins created a very difficult problem with which to begin his reign. Though the new viceroy could scarcely have learned of Hawkins's most recent depredations, he knew of his past voyages and he knew the law. Clearly the English were, at the very least, guilty of being in the Indies without the permission of the King, selling merchandise that had not been manifested at Seville, and trading without a license.[12] They obviously had to be removed and, if possible, arrested, but the means to this end were obscure. To begin with, though the forces of the viceroy were numerically larger, his fleet contained but two full-sized warships. In the *Minion* and his flagship, the *Jesus of Lubeck*, Hawkins possessed two vessels of more or less equivalent strength, and he had taken care to seize the shore batteries as well. A frontal attack was therefore impossible, and the prospect of remaining off an inhospitable coast in the face of a freshening breeze was no more attractive. The viceroy could only swallow his pride and accept the conditions proposed by Hawkins in the hope of achieving something at a later, more propitious, date. These were essentially that the Spaniards be permitted to anchor in a Spanish port provided that an exchange of hostages be effected and the English be permitted to control the islet to which the ships of both nations would have to be moored. Enriquez agreed to do this, albeit with some reluctance, and the new arrivals anchored in ominous proximity to the English.

Before two days had passed, close observation revealed that the Spaniards were secretly preparing an attack. Though Hawkins had expected this, and had indeed prepared for it himself, he registered an immediate protest. The viceroy's reply was reassuring and conciliatory, though notably unconvincing, and after a lapse of an hour or two, the covert preparations were resumed. The attack was launched at the dinner hour, and though the authorities differ somewhat as to the exact sequence of events at its beginning, there is little doubt about its end.[13] In close fighting with little room to maneuver their ships, the outnumbered but more heavily armed English were able to save only two vessels, and the men left on shore to hold the batteries were lost. Hawkins, who grossly exaggerated the false cordiality of his original reception, accounted this necessary ruse a piece of the basest treachery, a perfect example of inherent Spanish villainy.[14] The thousands of Englishmen who read his original pamphlet and Hakluyt's reprint of it apparently agreed.

This story needed no sequel, but a sequel there was in which treachery was compounded with cruelty, and cruelty with Popish fanaticism. In the process of clawing their way out to sea, the two surviving ships were able to save a number of crewmen from the rest of the fleet. Once off shore, they found that there were insufficient supplies for the trip back to England, and that some of the men would have to be set ashore in New Spain.[15] Among the hundred who volunteered to stay behind were Miles Phillips and Job Hortop. Both of these men left accounts of their capture and imprisonment by the Inquisition which, as indictments of Spanish cruelty, are far more effective than the testimony of Hawkins.[16]

The hazards involved in flouting the pretensions of the Spanish empire were even more vividly portrayed by the fate of the French colony in Florida. In 1564, a group of Huguenots, operating without the official knowledge of their king,[17] embarked for Florida under the command of René Laudonnière. An earlier expedition had deserted its post, and it was desired among members of Coligny's faction that the embryo colony be reestablished. Unfortunately, Laudonnière was unable to control his men, and thirteen of them embarked on a brief, if spectacular, career as pirates. After seizing a boatload of treasure and kidnapping the governor of Jamaica, they were arrested and taken to Havana for trial.[18]

Such effrontery could not long escape the attention of Philip II. True to his name, the "Prudent King" made inquiry into the official status of the French colony, and finding that it had none, resolved to extirpate what he could only have regarded as a nest of *corsarios luteranos*.[19] The man chosen to accomplish this task was a noble and capable soldier, Pedro Menéndez de Avilés. Arriving just as reinforcements came from France, Menéndez immediately attacked the colonists in spite of their numerical superiority.[20] Thanks to the consummate folly of the French in splitting their forces, he was able to capture the lot and hang them on the beach under a sign which read: "I do not this as unto Frenchmen, but as unto Lutherans and Pirates."[21] Others, chiefly new arrivals under Ribaut, simply had their throats cut.[22]

To the Spaniards, this was simple justice. The Frenchmen whose dangling corpses adorned the Florida beach were self-confessed heretics who had, by their deeds, proved themselves capable of piracy. Menéndez, who according to Merriman was a gentleman of the highest type,[23] thought of his task as the execution of common criminals, and on those grounds the Spanish Court defended him. As the French expedition lacked official sanction, its members were legally pirates. Furthermore, it was alleged that an attempt to return them for trial would have been suicidal in view of their superior numbers.[24] It was certainly not the sort of risk a prudent commander would take. The French themselves may not have agreed with this line of reasoning, but as the expedition had sailed without official sanction there was nothing for them to say. Laudonnière himself was not so reticent. After narrowly escaping from the Spaniards, he published an account of the whole affair in which he condemned both them and his followers while attempting to draw attention away from his own mismanagement. Hakluyt came upon it in Paris where he was acting as secretary to the English ambassador, translated it, and had it published under separate cover in 1587.[25] It has appeared in all subsequent versions of the *Principle Voyages*, and while its contents might serve to induce contempt for the French, its detailed picture of an unusually ugly massacre does little for Spain.

The denouement of this tragedy indicates that barbarism was not a Spanish monopoly. The conclusion of Laudonnière's narrative, which he divided into four "books," is devoted to a similar mission carried out by Captain Dominique Gourgues, who "most valiantly, justly, and sharply revenged the bloody and inhuman massacre committed by the Spaniards upon his countrymen in the year 1565."[26] Descending upon the small band of Spaniards still encamped at the site of the French colony, Gourgues hanged them under a sign which proclaimed, in grim parody of the original: "I do not this unto Spaniards, nor as unto mariners, but as unto Traitors, Robbers, and Murderers."[27] He must have thought this quite a touch.

As can be seen from this example, Hakluyt did not reject a horror story simply on the grounds that no Englishmen were involved. Even the poor Indians came in for their share of sympathy, though one wonders if this would have been the case had not Las Casas already called their plight to the attention of English readers. His hand is, at any rate, suspiciously evident in passages like the following:

If the Castilians, pretending a religious care of planting Christianity in those parts, have in their doings preached nought else but avarice, rapine, blood, death, and destruction to those naked and sheeplike creatures of God; erecting statues and trophies of victory unto themselves, in the slaughter of millions of innocents: doth not the cry of the poor succourless ascend unto the heavens? Hath God forgotten to be gracious to the workmanship of his own hands? Or shall not his judgments in a day of visitation by the ministry of his chosen servant, come upon these bloodthirsty butchers like rain into a fleece of wool?[28]

This was written by Raleigh's lieutenant, Lawrence Keymis, but those "naked and sheeplike creatures of God" sound very familiar indeed.

Others were more careful to acknowledge their sources. In his pamphlet on "The Last Fight of the Revenge," Sir Walter Raleigh cited Las Casas as a witness to Spanish cruelties in the New World, where, in Hispaniola alone, thirty thousand innocents were slain by their bloodthirsty masters.[29] His "Voyage to Guiana" is filled with horrified comments on the maltreatment of Indians, and he notes that in a single attempt to find an antidote to their arrow poison, the Spaniards "martyred and put to invented torture I know not how many of them."[30]

The experience of William Michaelson and William Mace, officers of the good ship *Dogge*, enabled them to draw the inevitable conclusion from all this. After exchanging honors with a Spanish ship in the Gulf of Mexico, they invited the Spaniards over to the *Dogge* for a parley and received in their turn a reciprocal invitation. When the English were safely on board the Spanish ship, the Spaniards leaped upon them, slaying the English pilot, and, as the authors say, "others were served of a like sauce." Had Michaelson and Mace not saved themselves by leaping overboard, they could not have warned all Englishmen to be circumspect in their dealings with "that subtle enemy, and never to trust the Spanish further, than that their own strength shall be able to master them; for whosoever shall through their simplicity trust their courtesy, shall by trial taste of their assured cruelty.[31]

As similar tales were repeated throughout Hakluyt's compilation, and as the English quite naturally tended to minimize their own brutalities, the reader was left, once again, with the impression that Spanish cruelty was unique. But in emphasizing the vein of cruelty and treachery which they claimed to discern in the Spanish character, Hakluyt's contributors were careful not to omit other traits, which, while odious in themselves, could also account for the presence of these shortcomings. Thomas Cates, in his account of the voyage made by Drake in 1585, tells of finding an escutcheon in the office of a Spanish governor which bore the motto *Non sufficet orbis*.[32] This discovery caught the imagination of later writers and the incident became nearly as famous as the man-eating dogs of Las Casas. Sir Walter Raleigh, an expert on ambition if ever there was one, made similar accusations. In his "Voyage to Guiana" he showed the chaos wrought in European chanceries by the gold and ambition of Philip,[33] but his concluding comments on "The Last Fight of the Revenge" speak directly to the point. After a storm scattered the Spanish fleet with considerable loss of life, he said: "Thus it hath pleased God to fight for us, and to defend the justice of our cause against the ambitious and bloody pretences of the Spaniard, who, seeking to devour all nations, is himself devoured."[34] As summarized by Lawrence Keymis, King Philip's aims were the essence of simplicity: "One law, one Lord, and one Religion, throughout the whole of Europe."[35] It was a remarkably acute observation. Philip's hatred of diversity was well known.

To the informed, however, these grandiose ambitions were but the manifestation of another all-pervading Spanish characteristic—greed. Anticipating a number of modern writers, the Elizabethans pictured Spanish colonial policy as little more than a frenzied search for treasure in which any method that offered the possibility of gain was readily condoned. Raleigh told of a chieftain who was led about in chains for seventeen days in the hope of gaining a larger ransom from his people,[36] while Keymis heard the Indians lamenting that the Spaniards had taken all their goods and then enslaved them.[37] Even Christianity was perverted to the service of mammon, and not only by the Inquisitors. John Chilton found friars telling the Indians that "with giving four reals of plate for a mass, they would deliver their souls out of purgatory";[38] and we have already seen that Raleigh, Keymis, and Hakluyt himself regarded Spanish religion as pure sham.

Was there no good in this people? Neither Hakluyt nor his contributors seemed to think so, for even the grudging admiration expressed by Williams and Churchyard is absent from these accounts. They are discouragingly uniform in their portrayal of a malignant and ill-favored race without a single saving virtue. Were not such a prodigy of nature incredible in itself, it might be admitted that Hakluyt was successful in endowing a political and economic crusade with high moral purpose. Certainly no one but the most skeptical of readers could feel guilty about seizing Spanish lands and property after perusing the *Principle Voyages, Traffiques and Discoveries of the English Nation*.

His literary executor, the Reverend Samuel Purchas, could claim no such distinction. *Purchas, His Pilgrimes*, though lengthy and even valuable in a documentary sense, was compiled with no discernible purpose in mind and offers no coherent picture of Spain or the Spanish colonies. It added some particularly grisly specimens to the gallery of Spanish tortures and did nothing to refute Hakluyt, thereby justifying its inclusion in this study; but it is essentially no more than twenty volumnes of assenting commentary presented to another, post-Elizabethan generation. The reign of James I saw successful English colonies planted in the New World for the first time, but the old ardent spirit seemed to be lacking, perhaps because James himself was determined to avoid trouble with Spain. The change is best demonstrated in an account written by Sir John Hawkins's son, Richard, of a voyage undertaken in 1593.

This narrative shows little of the directness that had characterized Richard's father. Young Hawkins, attempting to repeat Drake's circumnavigation of the globe, encountered endless trouble from his own men, largely because of his puritanical folly in caning them for bad language and other minor sins. If he spoke as he wrote, it is a wonder that he was able to survive at all, much less to captain a ship around the Horn; but somehow, bickering and complaining as he went, he managed to reach Lima before the blow fell. At this point, the Spaniards, who seem to have been awaiting him, gave chase. The seas were rough, and his pursuers were soon forced to give up the chase and return to port with splitting sails and a snapped mainmast. Instead of using this respite to make good his escape, Hawkins unaccountably lingered in the vicinity until the Spaniards repaired their ship and set forth a second time with the mockery of the townspeople ringing in their ears. Finally, in a battle off Guayaquil, the English were soundly defeated, owing largely to their own incompetence, but Hawkins characteristically preferred to blame all his troubles on a gunner whom he suspected of pro-Spanish sympathies.

The end of this comic-opera affair was surrender and imprisonment. Fortunately, as Spain and England were then at war, Hawkins was not regarded as a pirate. The Spanish admiral offered him generous terms, his own private surgeon, and comfortable quarters for the officers, making it possible for him to spend his captivity in abstruse legal disputes with the authorities. The conclusion shows that this kindness was not appreciated:

And can you forget how daily they abuse our noble natures, which being void of malice, measure all by sincerity, but to our loss? for that when we come to demand performance, they stop our mouths: Either with laying the Inquisition upon us or with delivering us into the hands of the ordinary justices, or of the Kings Ministers. And when urged with their promises, they shrink up their shoulders, and say, That they now have no further power over us. They sorrow in their hearts to see their promise is not accomplished; but now they cannot do us any good office, but to pray to God for us and to intreat the Ministers in our behalf.[39]

No discussion of the struggle between Spaniard and Englishman on the high seas would be complete without some mention of the expedition on which young Hawkins modeled his pitiable fiasco. The circumnavigation of the globe by Sir Francis Drake was perhaps the greatest single achievement of Elizabethan seamanship and a yardstick by which the success of other such ventures could be measured. It is surprising, therefore, to discover that no account of this feat seems to have been published by either Hakluyt or Purchas. Today, Sir Francis Drake is regarded as the greatest of the sea dogs. His exploits have been made the subject of endless romances, histories, and even television programs, but there is some evidence to suggest that his credit has not always been this good. The accounts of his doings in Hakluyt are remarkably sketchy, and Camden quite frankly despised him as a pirate.[40] His comment on Drake's most famous voyage is a piece of savage irony that tells how he returned

to the great Admiration of all men, and without any Crime laid to his Charge by his adversaries, but only that he had put Doughty to death, that he had left a Portugese whom he had taken upon the Coast of Africa to the Cruelty of the Spaniards at Acapulco, and had inhumanly set the Negro-maid before mentioned on Shore in an Island, after she was gotten with Child in his ship.[41]

The commendatory verses produced upon his return are called the product of an idle brain, and the usually gentle historian is pleased to note that many of Drake's gifts were spurned by the courtiers as the fruits of piracy.[42]

The "fullest" account of the expedition, written by its chaplain, Francis Fletcher, saw matters in a different light. Drake may not have been an avenging angel of the Lord, but in his chaplain's eyes he could not have seemed much less. No matter how great the outrage, one feels that Fletcher would have been prepared to defend it, provided that it had been committed by an Englishman. The Spaniards, by way of contrast, are flayed unmercifully, and instances of their ingenious cruelty are sprinkled liberally throughout the book:

> Yea, they suppose they do the wretches [the Indians] great favor, when they do not for their pleasure whip them with cords, and day by day drop their naked bodies with burning bacon, which is one of the least cruelties amongst many which they use against the nation and people.[43]

The result of this sadism, as Las Casas had long since pointed out, was that the "innocent and harmless Indians" were being barbarized to the great peril of the whites, who stood in constant danger of Indian attack.[44]

Though Fletcher claimed that the English were free of this unnatural vice, he unwittingly implicated them in another. His tales are a living mockery of those who would believe that avarice is the unique monopoly of Iberia, and he tells them with the smooth relish of an accomplished bandit. Two of these have been selected as examples of Drake's impact on a society so secure in its honesty that it did not trouble to guard its bullion.

In the first, a reconnaissance party comes upon a Spaniard sleeping beside several bars of silver. As Fletcher tells it, "we would not (could we have chosen) have awaked him of his nap: but seeing we, against our wills, did him that injury, we freed him of his charge, which otherwise would have kept him waking."[45] In the other, the English steal eight hundredweight of silver from a Spaniard who was carrying it by pack train. The comment is a masterpiece of misplaced courtesy: "we could not endure to see a gentleman Spaniard turned carrier so, and therefore, without entreaty, we offered our services and became drovers."[46] If this is a sample of the chaplain's humor, one shudders at the thought of the crew.

Obviously, the records of the Elizabethan seamen could have a double edge. To such reflective readers as Camden, these men might have much to answer for on the Day of Judgment, but to most people they were heroes. The glamour of their adventures is irresistible, and there must be very few boys in the English-speaking world who have not, at one time or another, imagined themselves upon the pitching decks of a galleon, broadsword in hand, scattering the murderous dagos right and left. The motives behind English expansion may have been mundane or even sordid, but the actions as recorded in Hakluyt and Purchas are the stuff of dreams. It was Spain's misfortune, at a time when English imaginations were being stretched to the outermost corners of the earth, to find itself enrolled as the national enemy.

CHAPTER VI. THE ARMADA

By 1588, the struggle in the Netherlands and the undeclared war in the Indies had driven Philip II to the limits of his considerable patience. Elizabeth's aid to the Dutch, though hardly decisive, had been irritating, and the situation on the Spanish Main was clearly intolerable. Hawkins had been succeeded by the far more formidable Drake, and Philip, plagued as ever by insolvency, found a major source of revenue imperiled by the Devonshire pirate. The descent on Nombre de Dios in 1572 and the famous circumnavigation of the globe, which yielded by some estimates nearly one half the annual value of the American mines, were typical of actions that could no longer be ignored.[1] And such minor Spanish successes as the hanging of John Oxenham at Lima could not obscure the fact that these raids were undertaken with the tacit permission of England's queen. As long as she remained unchastised, the Spanish treasure fleets would be in constant jeopardy. Such considerations, reinforced by Philip's abhorrence of heretics and his conviction that the Dutch would be more easily overcome if English aid were extinguished, led the "Prudent King" to hazard the most magnificent blunder of his entire career.

The defeat of the Great Armada has rightfully been regarded as one of England's finest hours, a national triumph from which its people have drawn comfort and sustenance in the darkest moments of their subsequent history. To many it has symbolized the moral and military superiority of the English nation, to others, the victory of Protestantism and liberalism over the powers of Roman darkness. Even cautious professional historians have seen in it the collapse of Spanish power and the beginning of England's supremacy on the high seas. All of these opinions have been debated at length, but whatever its wider implications, the Armada was certainly the high-water mark of English anti-Hispanism. Those who might have taken the stories of Dutchmen and sailors with a well-merited grain of salt could have no further cause for skepticism. The Spaniards had mounted a full-scale attack on England, and by so doing had proved themselves guilty of all the charges that had been laid against them. Had they not done so, the Black Legend in England might well have been stillborn and the bombast of the pamphleteers forgotten.

As it was, the old notions of Spain's criminal ambition to rule the world were confirmed. As Thomas Nashe expressed it, Philip seemed "about to devour all Christendom with invasion."[2] Equally important, the Armada provided the government and the Protestant faction with a new and unparalleled opportunity to muster public opinion against the enemy. Different motives were involved, but the end result was much the same. Spain stood convicted, not only of greed, tyranny, and ambition, but of two vices hitherto unthought of by earlier propagandists: cowardice and incompetence.

At first glance, this emphasis seems unaccountable. By minimizing the fighting ability of the Spaniards, our writers were at the same time diminishing the glory of those who had defeated them, but at that particular moment of English history the nation's leaders were concerned with far more pressing problems than the egos of Drake or Howard of Effingham. To begin with, the Armada was clearly not the end of the conflict with Spain. Not only Elizabeth and her counselors but the entrepreneurs represented by Hakluyt were sufficiently farsighted to realize that years of struggle lay ahead. The English people, brought up on tales of Spanish prowess, needed to be reassured that the failure of the Armada was not an isolated incident but a symbol of Spanish decay. Furthermore, it was thought necessary to convince the dissident Catholic community that they could expect no aid from Spain. It was these considerations that led Cecil to publish from his own pen *The Copy of a Letter Sent Out of England to Don Bernardin Mendoza*.[3] Claiming to be the work of an English Catholic addressed to the Spanish ambassador in Paris, it derided the Armada and declared the English Catholics loyal to the Crown. Likewise, Hakluyt, who as we have seen was anxious to minimize Spain's ability to defend its colonies, took the defeat of the Armada as his prime example. Much of his information was derived from Meteren, but other contributors, such as Raleigh, were quick to point out that "with all so great and terrible an ostentation, they did not in all their sailing round about England, so much as take one ship, Bark, Pinnace or Cockboat of ours: or ever burnt so much as one sheepcote of this land."[4]

Cecil and Hakluyt, in common with other writers of their time, implied Spanish incompetence by exaggerating the size of the invasion force. The failure of their "huge ships and mighty monarchies" to prevail over "the small pinnaces (as it were) of a tiny island,"[5] was regarded as significant. This myth has not yet entirely been laid to rest, in spite of the fact that in its extreme form it approached burlesque. Camden reported that the ships were so huge that the winds were tired of carrying them, and that the ocean groaned under their weight.[6] A Dutch writer asserted that Xerxes' fleet had been as nothing by comparison,[7] and Hakluyt permitted himself to wonder how the Spaniards expected to get such vast ships through the narrow waters of the Channel.[8] This is, of course, absurd; but the lie stuck. For centuries most people believed that the Armada was the larger of the two forces, and agreed with the poet who said of the battle: "Well guided little axes so force tallest oaks to fall."[9]

Ironically, this fiction was somewhat abetted by the Spaniards themselves, who, in an ill-advised attempt to terrify their enemies, published the Duke of Medina-Sidonia's official report on the condition of the fleet. Not only the ships themselves but their manpower and accoutrements were described down to the last pike and cabin boy with a veracity marred only by occasional optimism. Even today it is an impressive list, particularly to landsmen who could not have known that the ships were undermanned, undergunned, and short of ammunition, that the casks were green and defective, thanks to Drake, who had burned the seasoned staves at Cadiz in the preceding year,[10] and that much of the fleet's total tonnage lay in unwieldly, noncombatant cargo ships. Published in the major Continental capitals before the Armada sighted the Lizard, this document reached England only after the crisis had passed, and then in a form somewhat different from that approved by Madrid. Judging from the pseudonym of the translator, "Daniel Archdeacon," and from the prefatory epithets of one "E. B.," the Duke's report seems to have fallen among Puritans. Comparing Philip with Sennacherib, the introduction reminded its readers of Spanish cruelty in terms appropriated directly from Las Casas. As the "Spanish Nimrod" had hunted men with dogs in the Indies, so would he hunt Englishmen if given the opportunity.[11]

England's deliverance from such a peril could be explained in only one of two ways. Robert Greene gave voice to one possibility in his *Spanish Masquerado*:

> . . . none more glories in his Chivalry than the Spaniard: But I suppose his religion and stomach be equally poised: the one false the other faint, that what they attempt, is not to be overcome with prowess, but to suppress with multitudes: for their service in wars in either by policy to circumvent by perjury, to entail by treason, to undermine, or by some little martial practice to weaken the enemy, whom if they find valiantly to resist, their brave once cooled, they seldom or never dare give another Encounter. . . .[12]

This hypothesis was favored by Cecil, who had declared without a trace of shame that the entire Armada of 160 ships had been "furiously pursued" by 50 of the Queen's.[13] It was supported by the curious incident involving Don Pedro de Valdes.

Valdes was the commander of a galleass that surrendered without a fight early in the campaign. He was treated royally and remained in England for several years as a prisoner of war and pet of the courtiers. Why he chose this course remains a matter of conjecture, but his decision prompted Greene to ask: "Do the Spaniards prize life so high, that they make no estimation of honor?" Never the man to leave the answers to others, he concluded that the Spaniard's brags infer cowardly conclusions and compared Valdes unfavorably with Cleopatra, who did not suffer defeat so tamely but caused herself to be killed with an "Aspick."[14]

The other explanation was advanced in an unusually pious mood by Thomas Nashe:

> His Armadas (that like a high wood over-shadowed the shrubs of our low ships) fled from the breadth of our Cannons, as vapors before the Sun, or as the Elephant flies from the Ram, or the Sea Whale from the noise of parched bones. The winds envying that the air should be dimmed with such a chaos of wooden clouds, raised up high bulwarks of billowing waves, whence Death shot at their disordered Navy: and the Rocks with their over-hanging jaws eat up all the fragments of oak that they left. So perished our foes, so did the Heavens fight for us; *Praeterit Hippomenes, resonant spectacula plausa.*[15]

The notion that the victory was miraculous, or achieved through divine intervention, was widespread in an age accustomed to thinking in religious terms. It was given official status in a declaration which explained the seizure of Hanse ships for trading with Spain. Reminding the German merchants of their ingratitude, the Queen asked them:

> And if the victorious hand of God had not herein derided the cunning devises and purposes of the Spaniards, if it had not scattered so great a terror to all Christendom and drenched their carcases in the sea, what should the state of the said Hanse merchants have been?[16]

England's victory was, of course, no miracle. Had the truth been known by any save a few, it would not have seemed surprising. Medina-Sidonia, the Spanish admiral, thought so little of the expedition's chances that he repeatedly asked to be relieved of its command. His predecessor, Santa Cruz, had been little more optimistic. Even the squadron leaders, painfully aware of the inadequate preparations, are said to have shared this attitude.[17] It was not a happy or self-confident fleet that sailed from the Tagus in the spring of 1588, but the English could not have known this. Thanks to the ingenuity of their pamphleteers and the credulity of their historians, most of them never learned.

Such reflections may dispel the myth of Spanish overconfidence, and even the idea that divine intervention was needed to overcome the invader, but they do not answer the most important question of all: To what degree was incompetence and cowardice responsible for the Spaniards' defeat? Was the Armada "furiously pursued," and was its commander, as the *Letter to Mendoza* asserts, hiding throughout the engagement in a specially constructed shelter below decks?[18] The latter accusation can be quickly dismissed as mere calumny, but the former requires some examination. On the surface, it would seem that a fortnight's run from the Lizard to the Zeeland Banks indicates something less than a "furious" pace; but fortunately, there is more conclusive evidence available as to what actually happened. Medina-Sidonia's orders required, not that he decisively engage the English fleet and destroy it, but that he concentrate on making contact with Parma so that he might cover the invasion force on its journey across the Channel.[19] As the English had been able to seize the weather gauge, it was up to them to begin the engagement, but for nine long days they found it impossible to break what even Hakluyt was forced to call "a good and close order."[20] As Mattingly said:

After four battles—any of them, in ships engaged and shot expended, easily the greatest that had ever been fought at sea—there was no slack of Spanish discipline, no break in their formidable order, and the Spanish were as eager to shorten the range and come to hand strokes as they had been the first morning off Eddystone.[21]

As late as 1657, Samuel Clark could refer to this episode in the following terms: "All this while the Spaniards for want of courage, (which they called commission) did what they could to decline the fight."[22]

The story was somewhat different after the English used fireships in Calais roads, and there can be no question that the Spaniards were decisively beaten at Gravelines. The Armada was outsailed, outgunned, outnumbered, and outfought, but it is hard to justify the charges of cowardice and incompetence brought against it by the English pamphleteers.[23] Even after that last, decisive battle, the Spanish re-formed, and though almost entirely out of ammunition, offered to fight again.[24] The English, well aware that their work was accomplished, quite properly refused, and *la Invincible*, as the Spaniards wryly call it to this day, limped off to disaster in the Northern Sea. The King's original idea had been folly on the grandest possible scale, but it had been carried out with courage and dispatch.

The writers, as usual, did not show the forbearance of the English seamen. While Howard and Drake were graciously consigning their late enemies to the charity of unfamiliar seas and damaged ships, the pamphleteers began the gratifying, if unprofitable task of flogging the dead horse. As drowned Spaniards began to wash up on the Western coasts of Ireland, *Certain Advertisements*[25] proclaimed their losses and distress, while a pamphlet entitled *A Packe of Spanish*

Lyes compared premature reports of a Spanish victory with reality and railed at the contrast. Old accusations were revised in the new context and presented as fact. Chief among these was the ancient charge of cruelty.

Obviously, the Spaniards had committed no atrocities in their futile northern voyage, so it became necessary to conjecture about what they might have done, given the chance. The translator of Medina-Sidonia's report had included in his list of supplies a suitable, but wholly imaginary, collection of whips, chains, and instruments of torture with which the Spaniard would have amused himself if victorious. These spurious items captured the public imagination and led to much sensational comment, notably by the ballad maker and sometime novelist Thomas Deloney. During the battle itself he produced a song in which the Spaniards are accused of wanting

> To kill and murder man and wife
> as malice doth arise;
> And to deflower
> our virgins in our sight;
> And in the cradle cruelly
> the tender babe to smite.[26]

Now he brought forth another prodigy devoted to the Spanish whips and the purposes for which they were intended. Referring, like the preface of the Duke's report, to the tales of Las Casas,[27] and comparing the Spaniards to the Romans who raped and flogged Boadicea,[28] he described in bloody detail the fate that awaited English men and women at the hands of the invaders:

> One sort of whips they had for men
> so smarting, fierce, and fell,
> As like could never be devised
> by any devil in hell:
> The strings whereof with wiry knots,
> like rowels they did frame,
> That every stroke might tear the flesh
> they laid on with the same.

And pluck the spreading sinews from
   the hardened bloody bone,
To prick and pierce each tender vein,
   within the body known;
And not to leave one crooked rib
   on any side unseen,
Nor yet to leave a lump of flesh
   the head and foot between.

And for our silly women eke,
   their hearts with grief to clog;
They made such whips, wherewith no man
   would seem to strike a dog.
So strengthened eke with brazen tags
   and filed so rough and thin,
That they would force at every lash,
   the blood abroad to spin.[29]

This small sample of Deloney, though made up from whole cloth, is the Black Legend with a vengeance. A generation later these horrific imaginings were still being presented to an eager public by such figures as Samuel Clark,[30] but there was worse to come. An anonymous hack produced a *Skeltonical Salutation or Condign Congratulation and just vexation of the Spanishe Nation* to mock Philip on the occasion of his defeat. Suggesting that Philip is welcome to invade in such a manner any time he cares to,[31] he denounces the Spanish monarch, "That seeketh to nip us / To rob and strip us / And then for to whip us,"[32] and launches into one of the most amazing and tasteless discourses in the long history of popular literature. He is concerned, it seems, that trueborn Englishmen might cease to eat fish, knowing that the fish had feasted on Spanish blood. But he assures the reader that there is no danger to be apprehended from that quarter, because the fish, having digested the Spaniard, cannot pass along the venereal disease and other harmful elements found in his flesh![33]

The celebrated pamphlet of Petruccio Ubaldini is like a breath of fresh air in the midst of all this musky sensationalism. While its accuracy is anything but unimpeachable, it represents an effort at serious reporting, and was accepted by Camden and other writers. Its author, a Florentine settled in England, even goes so far as to excuse Spanish mistakes on the ground that a fleet composed of men of so many different nations, with different customs and languages, is at a great disadvantage however great and honorable its commander may be.[34] This is undoubtedly true, but Ubaldini presents no evidence that any serious confusion resulted from this or from any other cause save superior English seapower. Such a cavil, though, is no reason to damn a man for spreading prejudice. Ubaldini's real contribution to the Black Legend is an idle tale that has been repeated, and apparently believed, for generations.

During the days preceding Gravelines, one of the Spanish ships exploded mysteriously with heavy loss of life. As everyone who was near the powder magazine seems to have been killed outright, there is no way of knowing exactly what did happen; but Ubaldini, allowing art to gain mastery over truth, concocted his own version. According to him, a Flemish master gunner, incensed because a Spanish infantry captain had "according to the custom of that nation" dishonored his wife and daughter, laid a train to the magazine and fired it.[35] It is a good tale, worthy of an Elizabethan drama, but the absence of women in the fleet and the complete dearth of witnesses make it difficult to accept—even if one believes that rape is a Spanish national custom. At any rate, another tenuous link between the misdeeds of the one and the guilt of the many was forged.

If there is a moral to all this, it must be that as in so many cases today the early reports of an event are as perplexing to the participants as they are to future historians. Whether through design or genuine ignorance, the contemporary reader heard only of the cowardice, incompetence, and hypothetical cruelties manufactured by the popular press. They remained ignorant of what even Corbett, with his strong English bias, was forced to call heroism.[36] Thus the Armada, more than any other event, implanted anti-Hispanism in the English consciousness and introduced the new and fatal myth of Spanish incapacity. From the moment the great fleet slipped below the horizon, the consummate villainy of Spain, unredeemed by Divine favor, must have been obvious to all but the most avid of Jesuits. It was no longer necessary to develop new hatreds, but only to be reminded of old ones. Though the desultory and inconclusive war that followed possessed few features of interest, the chaotic situation in France provided frequent opportunities for recollection.

Spain's policy of alliance with the Leaguers against Henry III left it open to all sorts of accusations even before Parma's open intervention in French affairs in 1591. Typical of the general condemnation was a pamphlet entitled *The Coppie of the Anti-Spaniard made at Paris by a French man, a Catholique, Wherein is directly proved how the Spanish king is the onely cause of all the troubles in France.* The author, though forced to recognize the good services of the Huguenots and the contrasting perfidy of the Jesuits,[37] occupies a fairly consistent royalist position. In his battle against the Holy League and its Spanish backers Henry III found that his interests and those of the Protestants were remarkably similar. Only the succession of Henry of Navarre could satisfy his monarchical principles and provide security for the Huguenots. And this depended upon the defeat of Spain and its allies of the League.

Accordingly, the *Anti-Spaniard* saw the Leaguers as dupes of Philip's personal ambitions,[38] and pointed out what the French might expect from further encroachment, using the Sack of Antwerp, now fifteen years past, as an example. His countrymen are urged to prepare for the Spaniard's

insatiate avarice, their more than Tigerish cruelty, their filthy monstrous and abominable luxury, their wasteful burning of thy houses, their detestable ransacking and pillage of those great treasures which from all parts of Europe were laid up in store in thy sumptuous palaces, their lustful and inhuman deflowering of thy matrons, wives, and daughters, their matchless and sodomitical ravishing of young boys, which the demi-barbarian Spaniards committed in the presence of aged burgesses that were fathers, brethren, or husbands of those tormented patients, who to grieve them the more while they committed all these execrable villainies and outrageous cruelties, did tie and chain them at their bed's feet, or in other places, and last of all the general and continual cruel tormenting and massacreing of poor and wretched citizens.[39]

If, after perusing this passage, the reader still doubts that the Spanish are "the most savage, faithless, inhuman, and barbarous nation that the circuit of the whole world doth comprehend,"[40] he is asked once again to consider "the sack of the Indies" as told in Las Casas.[41] Fortunately, the author did not feel that France need accept the same fate. While the Spaniard is unquestionably guilty of every conceivable form of greed, cruelty, and perversion, he is also a great coward, a mere "bug-beare" incapable of making a respectable fight. For proof, one need look no further than his record in the present wars where he was seen but once, and then hiding behind the supply wagons,[42] or, in the Netherlands, where it takes him three years to take a city if he takes it at all.[43] Such cavalier references to the brilliant siegecraft of Parma attract little more than suspicion today; but to the Englishmen who had just defeated the Armada, they were probably as acceptable as the *Anti-Spaniard*'s musty accusations of Judaism and apostasy in the Spanish ranks.[44]

The *Coppie of the Anti-Spaniard* was perhaps the most vivid indictment to come out of the post-Armada period, but it was followed by a number of other, less comprehensive pamphlets telling of Spanish atrocities or setbacks while carefully avoiding all mention of Spanish victories. The accusations contained in them reflect an almost obsessive interest in the deflowering of virgins and in the supposed Jewish ancestry of the Spanish people. On the whole, they are dismal, repetitive tracts whose chief function lies in the reenforcement of existing prejudices. It is true that as the century progressed, Spanish military effectiveness declined measurably, owing partly to the adoption of Spanish tactics by other powers; but the very real failure of Spain's enemies to make inroads on its empire in spite of this was never stressed in the popular literature of the day. Thoughtful men may have wondered, if the Spanish were such fools, why the English expeditions of 1589, 1595, and 1598 were such signal failures; but if the press provides any indication, such thoughtful men were in short supply. The defeat of thirteen light Spanish galleys by five ships of the Levant squadron, superior in tonnage and almost equal in armament to the fighting galleons of the day, is accounted "shameful" by Hakluyt's reporter,[45] and even Sir Richard Grenville's stubborn defense of the *Revenge* is made to seem like a Spanish defeat when, of course, it was nothing of the kind.[46] When Essex's men took Cadiz, it was reported that "there was nothing more resolutely performed of the courageous English, nor more shamefully lost of the bragging Spaniard."[47] Though the English themselves were unable to retain the town, they thought the Spaniards should have been able to defend it for at least two months. The author concluded that the Spanish had either been rendered fainthearted by their defeats at sea, or were possessed of "a guilty conscience towards the English nation, for their dishonorable and devilish practises against her sacred majesty and the Realm."[48]

Similar statements are too numerous to recount in detail, but they are no less significant than the paucity of accounts in which the Spaniards emerge victorious. Throughout the remainder of Elizabeth's reign, English ships were seized and English raids repulsed, but neither Hakluyt nor the pamphleteers make mention of it. The closest they come to doing so is in a curious and suggestively titled report of the unsuccessful Portugal expedition of 1589: *A true discourse written (as is thought) by Colonel Antonie Winkfield emploied in the voiage to Spain and Portugall, 1589, sent to his particular friend, & by him published for the better satisfaction of all such as having been seduced by a particular report, have entred into conceits tending to the discredite of the enterprise and Actors of the same.* Whether it gave better satisfaction or not is doubtful. Though published both independently and in Hakluyt, it is a tale of woeful incompetence laced with incongruous charges of Spanish weakness and thinly veiled rumors of another attack to be made on England sometime in the near future. It must have served to keep the pot boiling, but the utter failure of the raid remains the best refutation of its main thesis.

Refuted or not, the charge stuck by virtue of mere repetition, and the legend of military incompetence persists today in spite of all evidence to the contrary. Infuriating to the Hispanists and misleading to Spain's enemies, it was, in England at least, a product of 1588. The legend of Spanish invincibility had been broken along with the last flimsy pretenses of amity. No matter how uninspiring the subsequent war, anti-Hispanism had reached its peak, and hereafter our story takes on an entirely different hue.

CHAPTER VII. TALES OF THE TRAVELERS

The Armada was the most important action of a war that alternately raged and smoldered for two long centuries. Not until Napoleon's day did Englishmen and Spaniards find themselves fighting in the same cause, and then only briefly. During that weary epoch new concepts of the Spanish character had little opportunity to develop, and a study of anti-Hispanism is forced to concern itself not only with origins but with the occasions on which those origins were recalled.

The one exception to this statement involves a phenomenon well known to the twentieth century. In any protracted struggle between two powers, people tend to develop an unwonted interest in their enemy and the society which produced him. This curiosity is largely hostile, aiming at the discovery of weak points, and is served by "experts" of one kind or another who profess an intimate acquaintance with enemy secrets. Everyone loves an exposé, and those prepared to offer one are assured of a public hearing. The ideological implications of the Spanish war ensured that a plentiful supply of such "inside" information would be forthcoming from those to whom consistency was no virtue, and who changed sides as conscience or necessity dictated. The motives of these men varied widely, but when they or their writings reached England, the burden of their sentiments was alike. This was only to be expected. Those who have taken the drastic and unpopular step of renouncing a nation or cause to which they had previously been attached must inevitably feel the need to justify their behavior. Even when their sincerity is beyond doubt, these efforts usually involve a condemnation of their old masters. Thus the men who turned against Spain united in exposing not only the country itself but its rulers and its religion as a monstrous fraud capable of any enormity. The most famous of these pilgrims was Antonio Pérez.

As protégé of the Prince of Eboli, Pérez had risen rapidly to a position of great trust and influence, soon becoming Philip's chief minister. His fall was as precipitous as his rise. For reasons known only to himself, he had attempted to play on the mutual jealousies of Philip and his brother, Don John, through the medium of the latter's secretary, Escobedo. When Escobedo arrived in Madrid, Pérez resolved to have him done away with before he could reveal the machinations which, by this time, had created an atmosphere of severe fraternal mistrust. Philip seems to have agreed to this stop, thinking that Escobedo was in some way responsible for Don John's disloyalty, and the unfortunate man was slaughtered in the street by ruffians attached to the household of Pérez.[1]

Pérez was not a popular man, and before long it was rumored that he was responsible for the murder. In the meantime, Don John died at his post in the Low Countries, and his papers convinced the King that his brother had been wholly innocent of the imputations made against him. Pérez was disgraced, arrested, and imprisoned. Thanks to the King's personal involvement in the affair, and his fear that Pérez would reveal state secrets if pressed too far, the fallen minister was accused only of peculation, though heresy was later added to the role of his crimes. Escaping, he fled to his native Aragon and became the center of a near revolt. When this project failed, he made his way to France and spent the remainder of his life haunting the courts of Western Europe in the hope of securing revenge against his former master. His intimate knowledge of state secrets made him dangerous for a time, but it was ultimately his propaganda efforts that damaged Philip the most. Two of these pieces, the celebrated *Relaciones* and a shorter, English-language work, the *Treatise Paraenetical*, were printed in London during the closing decade of the sixteenth century and contributed mightily to anti-Hispanism and to Philip's personal unpopularity.

The *Relaciones*, being published only in Spanish, are difficult to assess in relation to their effect on English popular opinion. Though the Elizabethan era produced both Spanish grammars and Spanish teachers, it is unlikely that knowledge of the language was widespread.[2] Of course, those who possessed such a knowledge were very likely men of influence as well as education. In any event, those who did read of Pérez's sufferings and peregrinations were treated to a smorgasbord of anti-Castilian anecdotes from which they could choose as taste or occasion demanded. While Pérez may well have been guilty of most of the crimes he was accused of, the merciless hounding of this ex-favorite is one of the more sordid episodes in King Philip's career. The exposure of his methods in the case could only do incalculable harm to his personal reputation and, perhaps by implication, to that of his country. Yet the *Relaciones* remain for the most part a monument to personal animosity rather than to national hatred.

Far more significant in the development of an English Black Legend, by virtue both of its being written in English and of its general argument, is a work which has unaccountably been neglected by modern Hispanists. Its title indicates its purpose: *A Treatise Paraenetical, That is to say, an Exhortation Wherein is showed by good and evident reasons, infallible arguments, most true and certaine histories, and notable examples; the right way and true means to resist the violence of the Castilian King: to break the course of his desseignes: to beat down his pride, and to ruinate his puissance.*[3] The use of the term "Castilian King" indicates more than the interesting but hardly surprising fact that even in the year of Philip's death Pérez was still maturing vengeance against his old employer. He seems by this time to have identified himself completely with the Aragonese enemies of Castilian rule and realized that by emphasizing Spain's internal dissensions he could best secure the cooperation of the English. Arguing that Philip's title to his realm was based on fraud,[4] he told of the hatred with which the King and his Castilians were regarded by other Peninsulars. As he expected this hatred to aid an English invader, he was careful to explain its origins, and in so doing penned an impressive diatribe, not only against Philip, but against Castilians as a whole. To him the latter are a "maligne and perverse" people, "full of pride, arrogancie, tyranny and infidelity," who, being descended from the Jews, are both traitorous and untrustworthy.[5] This racial approach is necessarily rare in Spanish literature, though it found favor among the Dutch and English who would have agreed when Pérez likened his enemies to Moors and accused them of apostasy whenever they came in contact with the infidel.[6] Presumably, he regarded the *Reconquista* as a fraud similar to those which had secure the hegemony of Castile, but without pausing to explain he hastened on to other accusations which are, in their way, even stranger to modern eyes.

His opinion of Philip, who "maketh no exception of persons . . . he poisoneth them all without fear of God or shame of man,"[7] had not improved in the four years since the appearance of the *Relaciones*; but he does seem surprised at another development: notwithstanding that "tyranny is as natural to Philip as laughter to a man,"[8] yet the more rascally of the Castilians take pleasure in his servitude.[9] Here the modern reader, far removed from an imminent attack by the *tercios* of Spain, must pause and consider. Perhaps this is the ultimate evidence of Spanish duplicity, for who could help but suspect a people who enjoy their servitude in "pride, arrogancie, and ambition"? On the other hand, it must be admitted that the Castilians were far more willing than their Aragonese brethren to surrender such ancient privileges as the right to strangle one's vassals without hearing their defense—a principle stoutly defended by Pérez during his abortive revolt of 1580.[10] In view of Pérez's attitude on this subject, it is not strange to find him horrified at the egalitarian spirit of Spanish justice which permitted "the least provost or marshall" to arrest the greatest lord.[11]

What the English thought of all this is hard to tell. The laudatory comments addressed to the peoples of Portugal and Aragon may well have had little effect on the popular estimate of Spain, for Spain to most Englishmen would have been synonymous with Castile. They knew of the difference between Castile and their old ally, Portugal, but all this talk of Aragonese, Galicians, Valencians, and what not probably served only to confuse them. Castile was the largest and most populous part of Iberia, master of the Indies, and the center of Spanish government. Its language and institutions dominated the empire, and for all practical purposes Philip himself was Castilian in outlook and temperament. An attack on Castile was therefore an attack on Spain itself, but in this case the attack might not have been as effective as Pérez hoped. His character and antecedents were not such as to inspire confidence, nor did his plans for attacking Spain generate wide enthusiasm at a court noted for its relatively common-sense approach to international politics. There was a quasi-official attempt to distribute the *Relaciones* on the Continent,[12] but other than that Pérez seems to have been ignored after the first flush of excitement had passed.

Much of this indifference arose from the defects of the man's own character. It has been argued, quite convincingly, that the character of Don Adriano de Armado in *Love's Labour's Lost* was intended as a caricature of the exiled Spaniard.[13] Shakespeare's description certainly fits:

> ... Our Court you know is haunted
> With a refined traveler of Spain,
> A man in all the worlds new fashion planted,
> That hath a mint of phrases in his brain:
> One, who the music of his own vain tongue,
> Doth ravish like enchanting harmony:
> A man of complements whom right and wrong
> Have chose as umpire of their mutiny.[14]

Like Armado, Pérez was elegant to the point of foppery, and addicted to the most outrageous hyperbole. He owed much of his personal unpopularity in Spain to the fact that

his humor is lofty, his discourse peremptory: his tongue filed, his eye ambitious, his gate majestical, and his general behaviour vain, ridiculous, and thrasonical. He is too picked, too spruce, too affected, too odd, as it were, too peregrinate, as I may call it.[15]

Such a man would be gravely suspect to the English, and, indeed, Shakespeare concludes with the fatal remark: "How you delight my Lords, I know not I, / But I protest, I love to hear him lie."[16] If this is the impression Pérez made on his contemporaries, he might fairly be disregarded were it not for the fact that he was cited as an authority by later writers. Moreover, his very presence may have done more damage than his writings, for Spaniards were rare in Elizabethan London, and it is altogether possible that he was taken as an archetype. Personal vanity and a lying tongue had already emerged as attributes of the stage Spaniard, and Pérez would have done little to discourage the myth. Whether he was believed or not, the "Pilgrim Spaniard" as he liked to call himself, could have done his country nothing but harm.

Pérez, of course, represented but one aspect of the turncoat problem. Thanks to a large and dissident Catholic population, England could rest assured that it too would lose a number of its sons to the blandishments of the enemy. As English Catholics were subject to heavy penalties and barred from holding offices of any kind, the more ambitious of them were forced to seek their fortunes abroad. In actual practice, "abroad" was Spain or the Spanish Netherlands. It could be argued that this migration was negligible, and that the Spaniards themselves regarded the exiles as untrustworthy; but it was nevertheless deemed necessary to print an exposé of the conditions under which the English expatriates were forced to live.

This unsavory task was undertaken in two closely related pamphlets, written by the same man and published in 1595. The first, *A Discourse of the Usage of the English Fugitives by the Spaniard*, is a much abbreviated version of a longer work published some months later and entitled *The Estate of the English Fugitives under the king of Spaine and his ministers*. Both are attributed to one "Sir L. L.," who has usually been identified with Sir Lewis Lewkenor, master of ceremonies to James I. Regrettably, Lewkenor was not knighted until eight years after these pamphlets were published, and Father Loomie further complicates the matter by ascribing them to a cousin, Samuel Lewkenor.[17] This is logical, as Samuel Lewkenor had served as a Spanish soldier in the Netherlands, but the only thing we know for certain about the author is that he claimed to be a repentant papist, lately in the service of Spain.

Taking his arguments from actual examples in the best tradition of Elizabethan pamphleteering, he tells of the suspicion in which the refugees, for all their Catholic loyalty, are held by the Spanish people. Abused and regarded as traitors, the English soldiers go in continual danger of being robbed and murdered by their Spanish comrades-at-arms.[18] Burnings, confiscations by the Inquisition, and tales in which friars cozen a dying merchant are used to wean the English Catholic from his faith,[19] while the more secular-minded are warned of the exhorbitant Spanish tax rates.[20] To those who would be interested in entering the Spanish service, he cites incidents in which others of like mind have lived in poverty on irregular pay or been hanged by the Dutch when the Spaniards refused to pay their ransom.[21] He concludes from all this that the Spanish are "the most base, wicked, proud, and cruellest nation that liveth,"[22] pagans at heart, or Moors, whose outward profession of faith is assured only by "the most cruel Heathen Inquisition."[23] This inner paganism, restrained only by fear, is exhibited in their characteristic "tyranny, blasphemy, sodomy, cruelty, murder, adultery, and other abominations," which are evident throughout their history, particularly with regard to the Indies and Portugal.[24]

One of those who failed to benefit by this sage advice was the elder James Wadsworth. Converted to Catholicism at Cambridge, of all places, he separated from his wife and small son, became a Jesuit, and ended as an officer of the Inquisition at Seville. In spite of this, his wife followed him to Spain, and his son was raised there as a Catholic. Upon attaining manhood, young James pinned his hopes on a position with the Infanta's suite, when that lady was to have been married to Prince Charles. When the marriage negotiations failed, he was sent to the Netherlands by Philip IV, but went to England instead, where he offered his services to the English Romanists. The rest of his career was spent in various unsavory doings, usually as a double agent and pursuivant, and finally as "a common Hackney to the basest Catchpole Bailiffs in Westminster." It was a sordid career, the monotonous duplicity of which was but little relieved by his literary efforts. These included a translation of Sandoval's *Civil Wars in Spain*, and two books in which he attempted to delineate the Spanish character: *The Present Estate of Spain*, and the *Further Observations of the English Spanish Pilgrime*. Both were published within a few months of each other during 1630.[25]

In fairness to Wadsworth, it should be stated that these books were primarily a meticulous description of the Spanish bureaucracy and court ritual. The comments on national character were almost an afterthought, encouraged, perhaps, by the fact that their author was writing them in a Spanish prison. Thus we find that the Spaniards "are full fraught with Complimental Verbosity: They hate duels, but often use private quarreling in the streets, and are much given to sudden and desperate stabbing: as also to Venery and Women."[26] But Wadsworth's memories must not have been all bad, for he recognized their quick intelligence, loyalty to their King, and love of horses.[27]

Even this meager praise was denied the Spaniards by Thomas Gage. The most vituperative of all the exiles, Pérez included, this renegade English Dominican may also have been the most influential. He was born into a famous Recusant family, but broke with them after his refusal to become a Jesuit. Posted to the Indies, Gage traveled extensively, and, according to his own account, became so disgusted with what he saw there that he returned to England and became a Puritan. His *The English-American his Travail by Sea and Land* is as bitter and vindictive as its author, but it is more than an indictment of Spain and Catholicism. Though chiefly concerned with clerical immorality, the maltreatment of the Indians, and the weakness of Spanish defense, the book provides a unique insight into the luxuriant growth that was Spanish colonial society. As so often happens, the hatred was grafted onto the basically healthy root of observant journalism, and serious readers were allowed to consume the one while seeking diligently into the other.

A reading of Gage, no matter how cursory, will immediately call to mind a host of other writers on things Spanish, many of whom were as yet unborn when he published in 1648. His treatment of the clergy, for example, is reminiscent of Voltaire and the eighteenth-century French philosophes. The American Church was never so severe as its Spanish parent, but even so, Gage's "disclosures" remain sensational in the extreme. It was his contention that the bulk of the friars in the New World had come thither to escape the rigorous discipline at home.[28] As a result, the Indians had been allowed to lapse into idolatry and worse.[29] To support this accusation he tells of several riotous evenings spent among the friars at Jalapa and Vera Cruz, where the time was spent in drinking, gambling, and blasphemy.[30] Even worse was the case of Brother "John Navarro," master and reader of divinity at Santiago de Guatemala. This worthy was caught in bed with a "chief gentlewoman" of the city and escaped only with severe wounds. The lady herself was slain by the offended husband, while the real villain of the piece, Navarro's brother, a friar who pandered in his spare time, was never brought to justice.[31] The tale may owe a great deal to the old *novelle*, but Gage was prepared to say that it was typical.[32]

In such an environment, it was only to be expected that lay morality would also be low. This was in fact the case, if Gage may be trusted. One of the most famous and widely quoted passages in this book deals with the apparel and carriage of the Mexican prostitutes and freedwomen:

And for the looseness of their lives and public scandals committed by them and the better sort of Spaniards, I have heard them say often who have possessed more religion and fear of God, they verily thought God would destroy the City, and give up the Country unto the power of some other nation.[33]

Such irregular domestic arrangements were the natural cause of brawls, duels, and murders, and even the most well-disposed were helpless to intervene.[34] When Las Casas's successor in the See of Chiapas attempted to repress the relatively innocuous habit of taking chocolate during Mass, the ladies of the district poisoned him with a box of candies.[35]

The whole of this corrupt society rested on the backs of the Indians, whose condition had not improved since Las Casas's day. We are told that the Spaniards amassed great fortunes by selling them drink at exhorbitant prices and working them to death in the mines and plantations. After retailing several instances of barbarous cruelty, Gage concludes: "These are but peccadilloes among the Spaniards, to make drunk, rob, and occasion the poor Indians death; whose death with them is no more regarded or vindicated, than the death of a sheep or bullock that falls into a pit."[36] And had their wealth and leisure purchased the colonists learning or culture? Gage's answer was devastating:

The Gentlemen of Chiapa are a by-word all about the Country, signifying great Dons (*dones*, gifts or abilities I should say) great birth, fantastic pride, joined with simplicity, ignorance, misery, and penury. These gentlemen will say they descend from some Duke's house in Spain, and immediately from the First Conquerors; yet in carriage they are but Clowns, in wit, abilities, parts, and discourses, as shallow-brained as a low brook.[37]

Clearly, such a society must have been wholly evil. But how much truth was there in Gage's accusations? There must have been great opportunities for clerical malfeasance, because Gage himself was able to accumulate a fortune of seven thousand pieces of eight in ten years of ministering to the unfortunate Indians,[38] but the writings of Sigüenza y Gongora and Sor Juana Inéz de la Cruz prove that Mexico was no cultural or religious vacuum. Perhaps it would be safest to say that Gage, like all of us, saw in retrospect what he wanted to see. He was by nature a scandalmonger, and his position in England, once he returned to his native land, must have been as insecure as that of any other recent convert. By 1648 a generation of men who had cut their teeth on tales of Spanish iniquity had seized power, and Gage's success in currying favor with them may be indicated by the fact that, as we shall see, Cromwell himself was influenced by his book. His purpose was to provide not only concrete and reliable information on the Spanish colonies but a moral justification for attacking them. According to the standards of evidence acceptable at the time, he succeeded in doing both.

The final figure in this gallery of pilgrims, exiles, and turncoats is so unlike the others that he may be taken out of chronological sequence and given a section all his own. The reason for this is that while Don Sebastian, King of Portugal, was a real human being, he was, as a pilgrim at any rate, wholly legendary. For our purposes, his story begins on the battlefield of Alcazarquivir, where he perished, together with the flower of Portuguese chivalry, in 1578. It had been a pointless expedition, badly led, and from all accounts Portugal would have been well rid of its young King had he not been childless. The succession passed to Sebastian's aged and infirm uncle, the Cardinal Henrique, and from him to Philip II of Spain. Philip's claim to the Portuguese throne was a sound one, but his accession in 1580 meant the end of Portugal's cherished independence. Nevertheless, the transition to Spanish rule was almost bloodless in spite of the fulminations of "Sir L. L.," who informed the English that the process had been accompanied by a wholesale massacre of the nobility and clergy.[39] This was, of course, unnecessary, as the remnants of the nobility had long since sold out to Philip,[40] but the settlement remained a standing source of grievance to the population as a whole.

It was in this bitter soil that the aberration known as "Sebastianism" first took root. Sebastian had been an unparalleled failure as a king, but he became the symbol of Portuguese independence; and even into the nineteenth century there were peasants who believed that, like the Welsh Arthur, he would arise when needed to smite the nation's enemies.[41] This legend arose from the fact that Sebastian's body was never returned to Portugal, and many patriots quite naturally refused to believe that he was dead. Such situations are a heaven-sent boon to mountebanks, and in due course no fewer than four imposters appeared to claim the throne. Of these, the least plausible was an Italian named Marco Tulio Catizone.

Catizone appeared in Venice in 1598 and rapidly convinced the more gullible Portuguese expatriates there that he was in fact their long lost King. Rumbles of these farcical doings reached England in the form of three pamphlets which told in some detail of the tribulations of Sebastian, since consigned to the galleys by the irate Spaniards,[42] and of the moral superiority if those Portuguese who had acknowledged his claims.[43] All of this nonsense was presented so as to cast the maximum amount of discredit on the cruel and treacherous Spaniards and their godless king, Philip III.

The author was a friar, José Teixeira, who had been engaged as a courier by Henry IV of France.[44] The first of his efforts contains a letter from one Giovanni Capugnano to Henry IV, telling of Sebastian's survival and of his imprisonment at the behest of the Spanish ambassador to Venice. This is followed by two letters from Teixeira to an unnamed bishop providing the same information and corroborating it with all sorts of testimonials, ancient prophesies, lists of characteristic birthmarks, and comparisons with the stupid tales manufactured by previous imposters. He concludes with a lame attempt to explain why the newfound king bears no physical resemblance to the departed, and cannot even speak Portuguese.[45] The second, and most important, pamphlet deals with the dastardly Spanish attempts to get him to commit suicide and, ultimately, his exposure on the back of an ass before being sentenced to the galleys.[46] Teixeira must have realized that this left much to be desired, for his final attack is little more than a paean of praise for Portuguese honesty and an exposure of the corresponding perfidy of Spain.[47]

Three hundred and fifty years later, with a wealth of documents at our fingertips, Teixeira's campaign may be seen as high comedy, but there is ample evidence to suggest that his readers thought otherwise. No one attempted to expose him in England, and English readers were left with the vision of a saintly Sebastian toiling in the galleys of the "Castilian King" while the devilish Spaniards gloated over their ill-gotten gains. Sebastianism agreed well with the doubts cast on Spanish sovereignty by Pérez and the "anti-Spaniard." As such, it found its way into later compilations of Spanish misdeeds and became an original, if relatively minor, ingredient of English anti-Hispanism.

On the surface, there is little to connect the five writers treated in this chapter. Widely separated in time as well as in their interests, their contributions are uneven in quality and significance. Whether, like Pérez and Wadsworth, they were the victims of their own duplicity or, like Gage, of obscure intrigues that have remained undisclosed, they all harbored a grievance against Spain and its monarch, and all posed as experts on the society they professed to hate. Even Teixeira falls into this category: a lonely wanderer, exiled for his adherence to the Prior of Crato.[48] Together, they offer us the picture of a decadent society in which all normal human values have been perverted through the influence of a corrupt and vicious court. It is the final element of the original Black Legend.

CHAPTER VIII. DIATRIBES UPON EMER-GENT OCCASIONS

With the accession of James I, the history of English anti-Hispanism entered a new and less virulent phase. Elizabeth had not been a particularly warlike ruler. Preferring policy to the uncertainties of open conflict, she was nevertheless capable of waging war when the occasion demanded it. The new king, on the other hand, was a pacifist to the core of his timid and scholarly soul. Born and educated in an atmosphere of unrestrained violence and brutality, he had learned to distrust the counsels of warlike men and to seek peaceful solutions even when they appeared unwise. He saw his own role as that of peacemaker and arbiter of the world's disputes, a kind of Solomon who, by virtue of his great learning and wisdom, could calm the unseemly passions of lesser men.[1] For all its egoism his was a noble vision, and it deserved better treatment than it has received from the nation over which he came to rule. With only a few exceptions his subjects neither loved nor understood him, and his reign was in many respects a personal tragedy. In no way was this more evident than in the failure of his most cherished hope: peace with Spain.

When James ascended the throne of England, he was precipitated into the midst of a war which, in its open form, was now more than fifteen years old. The struggle with Spain had not been decisive, and if Spain was nearing exhaustion, England seemed unable to deliver a final blow. Under the circumstances, James's readiness to negotiate was laudable. Thanks to his overwhelming desire for peace, England was spared the horrors of intervention in the Thirty Years War, and possibly of involvement in a general European holocaust. But when peace was finally declared in 1604, its announcement was greeted with an ominous silence in the streets of London.[2] The years of conflict had taken their toll, and as Godfrey Davies put it, "friendship with Spain—ran contrary to the prejudices of most Englishmen."[3]

Be that as it may, the sudden outbreak of peace meant a distinct check for the anti-Spanish writers. With Spain once again on technically cordial terms, James could not permit, much less encourage, the steady outpouring of anti-Hispanism that had been so characteristic of Elizabeth's reign. Typical of the new attitudes that Englishmen were expected to adopt were those contained in a pamphlet issued on the peace negotiations themselves. The author, Robert Treswell, Somerset Herald, pictured the Spaniards as bursting with good will,[4] which they evidenced by interceding for an English sailor who had been sentenced to hang by his own captain for striking a Spanish priest.[5] This optimistic view was shared neither by the officials involved[6] nor by the English clergy, who denounced the peace as a betrayal of Protestantism.[7] As Foscarini, the Venetian ambassador, put it in 1612, "the mass, both of nobles and people, desire war; nor is there any rank of person which conceals the satisfaction it would feel if leave were given for reprisals on Spain as in the time of the late Queen."[8]

As the reign grew older this discontent increased, reaching a peak of sorts during the brief Parliament of 1621. There were a number of reasons for this, not the least of which was that the treaty of 1604 had contained no assurance of free trade with the Spanish colonies, and the English still found their ships being seized on a variety of dubious pretexts.[9] Even more serious was the debate on the Palatinate, where James's own son-in-law, Frederick, was fighting for his life against a Catholic alliance headed by the Holy Roman Emperor. Popular opinion tended to believe that Spain was wholly responsible for this threat to Continental Protestantism and was furious with the King for refusing to intervene. Though anonymous tracts like *Tom Tell-Troath* began to tell him where his duty lay,[10] James was by this time past hearing. To patriotic Englishmen, the worst of all possible calamities had occurred: the king had fallen wholly under the influence of the Spanish ambassador.

Diego Sarmiento de Acuña, Conde de Gondomar, was one of the most fascinating and successful diplomats in history. At a time when Spain's military and economic forces were rapidly ebbing, he did much to neutralize his country's greatest rival through his personal relationship with the English King. This relationship now appears to have been much more complex than it did to contemporaries, who generally felt that the Ambassador simply dominated the King,[11] but there is little doubt that Gondomar used it to keep James out of the Palatinate and to forestall protests against the seizure of

English ships.[12] One of the means by which he accomplished these ends was to inveigle the King into a series of long and fruitless negotiations that aimed at an eventual marriage between the two royal houses of Spain and England.

Nothing could have been more unpopular than this "Spanish Match," as it was called, and when Parliament met in 1621 the honorable members made their views abundantly clear. Realizing that they could not appropriately interfere in the marital doings of princes, their debate ostensibly concentrated on the Palatinate. On November 27, Sir Edward Coke, taking his text from a pamphlet which appears to have been lost,[13] reviewed all the crimes committed by Spain during the time of Elizabeth. Not the least of these were the introduction of venereal disease and of a plague that affected sheep.[14] Sir Robert Phillips added that "the designs of Spain are ever accompanied with falsehood, being resting on that great Roman monster,"[15] and when another member rose to defend the House of Austria, he was "quickly stopped by the dislike of the House."[16] In the end, the Commons adopted a motion declaring their wholehearted support for intervention in the Palatinate,[17] but it made no difference. Frederick was forced to struggle along on his own, and the marriage negotiations continued. Convinced that the Commons were treading upon his cherished prerogative, James dissolved Parliament and temporarily imprisoned Coke and Phillips.[18] These questions, though, were by no means closed. To the intense disgust of the King, they were reopened in the popular press, active once again after nearly two decades in the wilderness.

The leading figure in this discussion was a clergyman named Thomas Scott. Regrettably little is known about this man, who must take an important place among contributors to the Black Legend. The account of his life in the *Dictionary of National Biography* seems to be largely fabulous, and even the details of his education are obscured by the multitudes of Thomas Scotts that infested seventeenth-century England. All we know is that in 1620, while rector of St. Saviour's, Norwich, he penned an indictment of James's policies entitled *Vox Populi, or Newes from Spayne*. The work was promptly suppressed, and Scott fled to the Netherlands, where he appeared in 1622 as pastor to the English garrison at Gorinchem. Shortly thereafter he was called by the English civilian congregation at Utrecht, where he served until his assassination in 1626 at the hands of a deranged soldier.[19] Throughout this period, he occupied his free time in the production of inflammatory pamphlets, and it is some indication of his fame that his own death was celebrated in a pamphlet entitled *A Brief and True Relation of the Murther of Mr. Thomas Scott.*

These details would remain unimportant were it not for the fact that Scott seems to have been under the protection of some powerful grandee at Court. When *Vox Populi* was first suppressed, the bishop of Norwich was asked to institute proceedings against the offending author. Instead, he introduced Scott's brother to the Archbishop of Canterbury who promised to do what he could on Scott's behalf.[20] In the end, Norwich was ordered to leave the pamphleteer in peace,[21] and the *Dictionary of National Biography* suggests that he returned to become the Earl of Pembroke's chaplain before fleeing once again to the Netherlands.[22] Thanks to the tragic loss of that gentleman's papers, this assertion cannot be verified, but Pembroke's well-known opposition to the so-called Spanish Party makes it a fascinating subject for conjecture.

Though Scott's political affiliations remain hazy, his aims were clear enough. Of the nine pamphlets with which we are concerned, three are personal attacks on Gondomar, four are monotonous catalogs of Spanish iniquities, and the remaining two are straightforward arguments in favor of intervening in the struggle for the Palatinate. *Vox Populi*, the first and most famous of them, falls into the first category. It is an ingenious and wholly imaginary account of a *residencia* held in Madrid upon Gondomar's return from England. All Spanish officials were subject to these courts of inquiry upon completion of their terms in office, and in this case interest centers around what Gondomar has done to advance his master's claim to universal sovereignty.[23] It turns out that he has done quite a bit. In addition to setting the King and Parliament at loggerheads and introducing the vexed marriage question, he claims to have caused Raleigh's execution, prevented the English from sending forces to

Venice, and convinced them to withdraw all effective support from the United Provinces.[24] Mention of the proposed marriage sets off a lively discussion on the merits of that particular scheme, and Gondomar is forced to defend it as the best means of weakening England. The only difficulty he foresees is that, with the exception of the more rabid papists and the "begging and beggarly" courtiers, all England is vehemently opposed to the union.[25] Though he has succeeded in having the anti-Spanish preachers suppressed,[26] much remains to be done.

So popular was this dramatic little fiction that it was reprinted in 1659, and again in 1679, in connection with the "Popish Plot." Gondomar also figured in another of Scott's works, published in 1624. *The Second Part of Vox Populi, or Gondomar appearing in the likeness of a Matchiauell*, is, like its predecessor, cast in the form of a round-table discussion, precipitated in this case by Prince Charles's angry departure from Madrid after the final breakdown of the marriage talks. In it, the Spanish politicians discuss why the English are so ill-disposed to them and outline a plan which is based on keeping the English peaceful while their country is subverted from within. The consequent soul-searching reveals that while Scott's form is revolutionary, the matter is not. The Spaniards obligingly accuse themselves of having Moorish blood, using English friendship as a stalking-horse, and of calling up not only the Armada but the Gunpowder Plot.[27] Gondomar waxes philosophical:

> Some think that there is a natural antipathy or contrariety between our disposition and theirs, they living in the North, and we in the South; which being (as Charron a French Author observeth) nearer to the Sun, the inhabitants are more crafty, politique, and religious . . . even to superstition and idolatry, whereas on the contrary, those of the North (howsoever goodlier in person, better faced, and more beautiful than ourselves by reason of the coldness of the climate, preserving inwardly the natural heat and radical moisture) are plain simple, nothing as religious withall, of the glorious ceremonies of our Church.[28]

Obviously, the Nordic fantasy of racial superiority was already abroad in 1624! Scott atones for this only partially when he has Gondomar say that the anti-Spanish pamphlets "proceed from the

pens of light and unstayed wits," flatterers, time-servers, and op-
portunists.[29]

In these two earlier pamphlets, Scott regards the Spanish ambassador as a dangerous schemer and an appropriate mouthpiece for
atrocious sentiments, but in his tale of Sir Walter Raleigh's ghost,
he descends to vicious personal abuse. Published in the last year of
Scott's life, *Sir Walter Raleigh's Ghost: or England's Forewarner*
is satire in which the wit has been overwhelmed by bitterness. The
scene opens in a garden, where Gondomar has gone to meditate on
his evil plans for England. He is alone, "lest his antic postures,
mumps, moes, and monkey-wry faces might draw laughter, or scorn,
from his vassals.[30] Suddenly, Raleigh's shade appears and taxes the
astonished villain with a list of Spanish crimes ranging from the
Armada to the imprisonment of Don Sebastian.[31] Panic-stricken,
Gondomar throws himself to the ground, confesses his admiration
for an equally long list of well-known criminals, and calls himself
"the very nose of the Spanish state, through which hath been voided
all the excrements, both of the head and the whole body."[32] Not to
be outdone, Raleigh interrupts from time to time with even more
opprobrious insults.

The Spanish crimes outlined by the ghost in his confrontation
with the cringing Gondomar had already formed the basis of four
other pamphlets. Though not nearly so picturesque, these are of
greater importance to anti-Hispanism because they presented a complete and lucid, though wildly biased view of recent history. According to the most important of them, the *Vox Coeli*, Spanish offenses against England began in the days of Pedro the Cruel and
the Black Prince.[33] This curious conclusion is reached by a committee composed of the past rulers of England, presided over by Henry
VIII. These worthies, Queen Mary included, agree that the Spaniards were responsible not only for every plot attempted by anyone
during Elizabeth's reign but for the murder of Henry III and Henry
IV of France, of William of Orange, and, once again, of poor old
Don Sebastian.[34] Moreover, they had received "Rome's hellish and
bloody Inquisition,"[35] subverted Barneveld in the Netherlands, and
sown discord among the Swiss.[36] Their record in the Indies was even
worse. That paragon of gentleness, Henry VIII, is made to declare:

How it hath both grieved and amazed me to understand how at Cuba, Haiti, Peru, Panama, and Mexico, and in all those vast isles and spacious continents, that the Spaniards with a more than hellish cruelty, have slain such infinite millions and miriads of those poor Indians, whereby in a manner they have wholly depopulated these populous countries and not only made rivers but whole seas of their blood; and of whose inhuman and bloody cruelty I may justly say; that as all former ages cannot show the like precedent, so our posterity will difficultly believe it.[37]

All of this is interspersed with such homilies as "The Spaniard is by nature, as treacherous as proud"[38] and "To trust to Spain is to rely on a broken staff, and to harbor a serpent in our own bosoms."[39] The discussion closes with a long indictment of Gondomar's pernicious activities and further warnings against the Spanish Match.[40]

Similar conclusions are to be found in *Robert Earl of Essex his Ghost*, published, like *Vox Coeli*, in 1624. Essex argues against the Spanish marriage on the ground that the Spanish royal family is "an incestuous generation"[41] and that James should dissolve all treaties with those "Romish wolves and Spanish foxes, who have devoured so many of Christ's sheep, and laid his vineyard to waste: Yea, the blood of the Saints doth continually cry at heavens gates for vengeance."[42]

Presumably, the vineyard in question is that of the Netherlands, for in a later appearance, this time in 1642, Essex's spirit recommended a close reading of the Dutch chronicles.[43] Fortunately, the reader did not have to wait until the outbreak of civil war brought the censors to nought. Even before the publication of *Vox Coeli*, Scott had written two tracts dealing specifically with the history of the Netherlands. The first, *Newes from Pernassus*, is a rather clumsy, involved, and disorganized allegory involving Spain's plea before the throne of Apollo to heal the open sore of the Netherlands. The other, a well-conceived dialogue between two soldiers, one embarking to fight for Spain and the other for the Dutch, is much more effective. Like *Vox Populi*, the *Tongue-Combat*, as it was called, gives a superficial appearance of impartiality, but the pro-Spanish soldier ultimately gets the worst of it. There is a lengthy recitation of Spanish atrocities in the Netherlands, and numerous references to Las Casas, the abortive French colony in Florida, and the various fulminations of Sir Walter Raleigh. Spain's superiority in Europe is once again traced as the product of fraud, and the Spaniards' willingness to tolerate such traitors as Sir William Stanley, who betrayed Deventer is said to be proof of their Moorish and Jewish blood.[44]

Scott was very much at home in this sort of quasi-historical argument, and he found it difficult to abandon even when the occasion demanded something quite different. His *Certaine Reasons and Arguments of Policie, Why the King of England should hereafter give over all further Treatie, and enter into warre with the Spaniard* may be taken as an example. In theory, at least, he was attempting to convince James that war would be advantageous for reasons of state, but he is finally forced to rely on the same tired historical complaints that could never have impressed a man of James's undoubted learning. The King had his faults, but neither vindictiveness nor ignorance were among them, and Scott was unquestionably playing on both. This tendency reached a climax of sorts in his *Experimental Discoverie of Spanish Practises, or, The Counsell of a well-wishing Soldier*. This sorry exercise has been universally attributed to the unfortunate Scott, though if it is indeed his the quality of writing and scholarship is far below anything else he attempted. It is weighted down with invective and larded with dubious citations. Guicciardini is quoted as saying: "The Spanish Nation are covetous and deceitfull, and where they be at liberty, exceeding outrageous, tyrannous, and very proud and insolent." The origins of this remark are as difficult to uncover as those of the statement attributed to one "Andrew, a famous Senator of Venice," who declared, that "they are unfaithful, ravenous, and the most insatiable of all Nations: For where is it (saith he) of all the places of the world, where these infamous Harpies set their feet, which is not defiled with the foot steps of most abominable vice." We should not be surprised that the man who called the Spaniards "loathsome Swine, thievish Owles, and bragging Peacocks" remains entirely anonymous.[45]

Unlike most of Scott's writings, the *Experimental Discovery* focuses its attention on the West Indies to the exclusion of the Netherlands. There are tales of Spanish cruelties taken from Purchas,[46] and the inevitable reference to Las Casas:

... the world of America was not so much unknown to the former ages, as their monstrous and new devised cruelties, which these devilish and tyrannous Spaniards have inhumanly practised amongst the simple and innocent people, as appeareth by Don Bartholomew de Las Casas Bishop of . . . and other of their own historiographers.[47]

Altogether it is a most unsatisfactory performance, and one with which Scott might well have been ashamed to be associated.

An assessment of Scott's contribution to the Black Legend is by no means an easy task. Obviously, he dealt with a great number of subjects and, for the most part, dealt with them effectively; but they were all subjects which had been dealt with before. Gondomar was a new grievance, and his attempt to blame the Spaniards for the Gunpowder Plot[48] enjoyed a brief and limited success, but primarily he was a collector of other men's anecdotes. His reliance on Las Casas and the Elizabethan pamphleteers has been remarked upon ad nauseam, as have his monotonous catalogs of dead and dubious sins. We must conclude, therefore, that his achievement was negative in more than the usual sense. Thomas Scott was the greatest of those who, without adding much in the way of new material, interpreted anti-Hispanism to a new generation. He did so with great originality and a modicum of wit, and there is every reason to believe that his influence was great. Gardiner claims that the *Vox Populi* was widely believed as true history,[49] but whether it was or not, Scott crystallized the hatreds and frustrations of a people who still longed for revenge and the secure establishment of Continental Protestantism. King James's ineffectual attempts to stop him were not wholly unjustified.

For all his overwhelming preeminence, it would be wrong to assume that Scott stood alone against the King and Gondomar. Others attempted to make themselves heard, but with the exception of *Tom Tell-Troath* and one or two others their efforts went unrewarded by print. The *Somers Tracts* are filled with manuscripts that reflect deep concern over the Spanish Match, the Palatinate, and the growing influence of the pro-Spanish party at court. Owing to the vigilance of James's censors, most were circulated privately, if at all. One exception was a play by Thomas Middleton, published in Leyden under the title *A Game at Chesse*. It is a masterpiece of dull allegory in which Prince Charles, predictably cast as the "White Knight" checkmates the "Black King" by discovering that the marriage negotiations are aimed at the destruction of England. By comparison, Scott seems a model of levity and wit!

Meanwhile, the King's failures were coming home to roost. Prince Charles and his erstwhile companion Buckingham may not have believed that the marriage negotiations were intended to destroy England, but they soon saw that the Spaniards had no intention of bringing them to a favorable conclusion. Furious, they returned to England, blissfully unaware that by their foolishness in going to Madrid they had given the Spanish a heaven-sent opportunity to make off with what little remained of England's independent foreign policy. The mind boggles at what might have happened had Olivares decided to lay hands on the aging King's favorites, but perhaps his did too, for "Steenie" and "Baby Charles" made their way back to James unharmed. Time was to prove that neither of them was an intellectual giant, and their first actions upon returning proved it. To the delight of the Commons, they added their voices to those demanding war. Overnight the despised Buckingham became a national hero,[50] and plans were set on foot that were to lead to one of England's more deplorable military catastrophes.

The Cadiz expedition of 1625 was a failure in nearly every way and, as such, was of little interest to the popular press. Victories were wanted, and as none were forthcoming the pamphleteers were forced to derive what comfort they might from triumphs of a more personal nature. The most notable of these was the extraordinary adventure of Richard Pike.

Pike (or Peeke, as it was sometimes spelled) was a native of Devonshire who accompanied the expedition as a foot soldier. One day, while foraging for oranges, he was attacked by a Spanish horseman, whom he soon unhorsed and defeated. By his own account, this trueborn English hero then attempted to rob the fallen Spaniard but was prevented from doing so by the untimely appearance of fourteen Spanish musketeers who seized him and bound him securely for removal to the jail at Jerez. No sooner was this accomplished than the first Spaniard, recovering from his fright, set upon the helpless Pike and tried to kill him before the musketeers could intervene. To Pike, this was unpleasant, but not surprising, for in his own words, "I too well knew that the Spaniard is haughty, impatient of the least affront; and when he receives but a touch of any dishonor, disgrace, or blemish (especially in his own country, and from an English man) his revenge is implacable, mortal and bloody."[51]

Thanks to the good offices of the other Spaniards, Pike survived this murderous assault with nothing more than a severe cut on his face and was immediately taken to Jerez for interrogation. His answers were so deliberately offensive that he was quickly involved in a duel with one of his interrogators. On the appointed day, with his wound as yet unhealed, Pike disarmed his opponent before a large audience. With his blood at full boil, he then offered to fight any three Spaniards there present, if only they would provide him with a stout English quarterstaff. This was quickly done, and three swordsmen advanced to their doom. According to the account, Pike killed one and disarmed the other two in a matter of seconds, to the great astonishment of the local nobility, who protected him from the crowd and sent him to Madrid to be presented to the King. Though treated with great generosity and offered a commission by Philip IV, Pike preferred to return to his native land, and it is a credit to the Spaniards that he was immediately allowed to do so.

This story seems to have created a minor sensation in England, and if there is any truth in it at all Pike deserves the encomiums he lavished upon himself. His adventures were retold in a ballad,[52] and in a play entitled *Dick of Devonshire*, which does not seem to have been performed. It may have been that its author was not sufficiently anti-Spanish for the temper of 1626. While he tells of Pike's doings and includes a dark tale in which the villainous Spaniard Henrico rapes his own fiancée and then refuses to marry her, he also points out that "the hate a Spaniard bears an Englishman / not natural is nor Ancient," but springs from readily ascertainable historical causes.[53] Pike's own version was more acceptable because he supplemented it with tales of horror. He may have been a brave man, but he neither loved nor respected his enemies and was only too happy to discredit them with incidents in which the English,

before they Knew their own danger, had their throats cut. Some had their brains beaten out with the stocks of muskets; others their noses sliced off; whilst some heads were spurned up and down the streets like footballs; and some ears worn in scorn on Spanish hats. For when I was in prison in Cadiz, whither some of these Spanish *picarros* were brought in for flying from the Castle, I was an eye witness of Englishmen's ears being worn in that despiteful manner.[54]

As the ill-equipped and badly commanded English were more often surprised than victorious in this campaign, it must have been difficult to find enough satisfactory news. The only other British triumph reported at this time was that of Captain Quaile, a privateer of Portsmouth. Quaile and his thirty-five crew members succeeded in sacking an unnamed village in Galicia by the simple expedient of pretending to be French mariners in distress. When the towns-people came on board to help them, they were locked below decks while the English went ashore. The author suggested that this was the proper course to follow in subduing that "potent and bloody enemy" and retold Pike's story as that of a Lisbon merchant who tired of his Spanish companions and their endless bragging.[55] The only novelty in all this is that one Englishman, at least, was now prepared to admit that Spain was a "potent" enemy.

Before the Cadiz expedition actually sailed, James I died, his fervent hopes for peace confounded by the pride of his son and the prejudice of his people. His successor began an inauspicious reign with Spain once again in her usual post as national enemy. It should have been the signal for a new outburst of anti-Hispanism on the Elizabethan model, but for a variety of complicated reasons the fury never really broke. In the first place, the war did not flourish, even by the modest standards of the 1590's. Buckingham's gross misman-agement had reduced him to his accustomed level in the popular esteem, and the Commons were refusing to grant subsidies as long as he remained in command.[56] Moreover, by 1627, England had added France to its list of active enemies through the seizure of

French ships bound for the Spanish Netherlands. With administrative chaos prevailing in an unpopular government, and two major enemies to choose from, the Elizabethan unity of purpose was not to be hoped for.

Several pamphlets and ballads appeared during this period, but only one possesses any real originality or interest. This was a curious work called *Miles Gloriosus, the Spanish Braggadocio: Or, the humour of the Spaniard*. Translated from an original version published in both French and Spanish in 1607, it lists forty-seven "brags" that call to mind the verbal excesses of Mike Fink and Davy Crockett. They revolve, as such things usually do, upon the braggart's prowess in bed and battle and contain such gems as "when I walked I made the earth to tremble with the abundance of my strength, the heavens were afraid, the winds ceased, and the sea became calm."[57] Many of them are highly amusing, but it is doubtful that the English reader would have taken them in the spirit with which they must originally have been written. The dedication makes it perfectly clear that the collection is to be regarded as evidence of Spanish conceit.

As the reign of Charles I drew to its tragic close, Englishmen became more and more immersed in their own internal problems. Then, if ever, Spain should have been left alone, but in 1642, when the conflict between King and Parliament was taking on the somber colors of a civil war, a new and virulent rash of anti-Spanish pamphlets appeared in the bookseller's stalls. As with so many events in the early Stuart period, the reasons for this seemingly illogical outbreak are almost "metaphysical" in their obscurity. For once, Spain had done nothing to offend either the sensitive Protestants or the populace at large. Distracted by rebellions in Portugal and Catalonia, and plagued, as ever, by insolvency, Spain's behavior upon the wider European stage had been less offensive than at any time during the preceding century and a half. This fact was recognized in the pamphlet, *Englands Present Distractions Paralleled with those of Spaine and other forraine Countries*, but it did not prevent a long recitation of Spanish crimes against the Netherlands,[58] or the appearance of several pamphlets that had originally been written against the Spanish Marriage. All aimed, indirectly, at discrediting the Stuarts. Thomas Allured, in his *Copie of a Letter Written to the Duke of Buckingham*, argued that all those who sought to ally themselves with Spain, by marriage or otherwise, would bring themselves or their progeny to a bad end,[59] while Thomas Scott's hitherto suppressed sequel to *Robert Earl of Essex his Ghost* reminded Englishmen that their escape had been a narrow one. One anonymous writer embarked upon a long list of Catholic plots, including over a dozen for which Spain was responsible, in an attempt to convince his readers that Charles's well-known tolerance for Catholics was a menace to the state.[60] Even the author of *Englands Present Distractions* had an ulterior motive in mind. In his opinion, the Catalonian revolt could be compared with that of Ireland, and the tyranny of Strafford with that of Juan de Mascarena. Both, of course, were the mere instruments of "the unlimited and infinitely ambitious power of the Clergy."[61]

It is clear from this that hatred for Spain was already so deeply engrained in the English mind that it could be used as a stick with which to beat an unpopular ruler. If further proof is needed, one need only look at the pages of Sir Anthony Weldon or Arthur Wilson. Like the printers who revived anti-Hispanism in 1642, their purpose was to examine the deeds of the Stuarts in the light of Puritan sympathies. Weldon, who was chief of the parliamentary committee in Kent during the troubles,[62] was primarily concerned with the shame incurred by the English in their attempts to secure peace with Spain. His version of the peace talks in 1604 is quite different from the recollections of Somerset Herald. According to Weldon, the Spaniards served the English ambassadors roast meat,

yet they did beat them with the spits, by reporting that the English did steal all the plate, when in truth it was themselves, who thought to make hay while the sun shined, not thinking evermore to come to such a feast, to fill their purses as well as their bellies, (for food and coin be equally scarce with that nation).[63]

This slur was avenged when Sir Robert Mansell caught a Spaniard stuffing his doublet with plate,[64] but later on another Spaniard stole Mansell's hat, which contained a valuable jewel, and hid in the courtyard of an *alguacil*. When Mansell demanded that his hat be returned, the *alguacil*, though an officer of the law, wanted to keep the jewel for himself and set the thief free.[65] Weldon was even more incensed because the Spaniards had used Prince Charles as a private person,[66] apparently forgetting that that was how he had been introduced in Madrid.

Wilson, on the other hand, was opposed to peace with Spain on more general grounds. A large, violent man, he believed that "there was no theme for history when men spill more drink than blood."[67] He regarded Gondomar, "that insinuating minister," as a genuine menace but was more angry with the foolish king and his corrupt courtiers who gave that master of "cunning practices" an opportunity to set his snares.[68] His only venture into gratuitous anti-Hispanism occurs when he anticipates the modern textbook writers by declaring: "The Spaniards, the first discoverers [of America] being more covetous to grasp, than well able to plant, took possession of the most precious places."[69]

These observations lead us into the aggressive anti-Hispanism of Cromwell's day, when Englishmen, freed from the policies of the Stuarts, could once again devote themselves to raiding the Spanish Main. But in the meantime, what can be said of the anti-Spanish feeling that appeared at such well-defined intervals during the reigns of James I and his son? On the surface, it appears to be little more than the evanescent product of the specific crises in which it appeared, a mere will-o'-the-wisp, wholly lacking in the splendid unity and sense of purpose that characterized its predecessor.

To some extent, such a view may be correct. Stringent censorship and the refusal of the Crown to sanction new anti-Spanish projects ensured that the campaign begun under Elizabeth would lose much of its momentum. During the whole first half of the seventeenth century only Gondomar and the rather hesitant references to the Gunpowder Plot relieve the general tedium of our summary. No, the real interest in this period lies not in what was newly brought to light but in what was remembered. The harsh reception accorded to the peace of 1604 and the widespread distrust of a "Spanish Match" indicate that the Elizabethan writers had accomplished their task. In 1580, the Puritans and those interested in overseas trade had hated Spain, but there is little reason to suppose that the majority of their countrymen cared one way or another. Forty years later, it was only necessary to remind the sons of what the Spaniards had done, or tried to do, to their fathers.

From another point of view, the anti-Spanish writings of 1603–1642 may well have been what they pretended to be: a counsel on the state of public opinion, published not for the people but for the better guidance of the King. This interpretation has much to recommend it, though I doubt that pamphleteers have ever aimed at so narrow an audience. In either case, the conclusion is the same. The enemies of Spain, now numbering, in all probability, the majority of the English people, were lying in enforced quiescence, awaiting the dawn of another day. Anti-Hispanism had ceased to be a matter for special pleading and had become a major current in the thinking of a multitude. The pamphlets we possess, for all their rarity and their apparent defects, mark where, following the course of least resistance, this current came bubbling to the surface.

CHAPTER IX. THE FRUITS OF HATRED

On January 30, 1649, King Charles I of England died on the scaffold at Whitehall. The crowd, whose passions were to no small degree responsible for his being there, are said to have given a mighty groan. Perhaps they sensed that more than a king had perished in the shadow of Inigo Jones's Banqueting Hall. It was one of the great moments of history, and one likes to imagine that Oliver Cromwell too appreciated it as such. In all probability he did, for his own dramatic instinct was unerring—a quality that has tempted many to refer to him as a latter-day Elizabethan. This judgment may be irrelevant. It is certainly superficial, for men of Cromwell's stature cannot be so easily typed. Imbued with some inner power beyond reason, they transcend in their own minds the laws set down for ordinary mortals. But in one aspect of his being, Cromwell can be accused of truly mirroring the Elizabethan spirit: his deep and abiding hatred of Spain.

We have already seen how, in the reigns of Charles and his father, the Black Legend began to bear fruit as its message sank into the minds of Englishmen. By the time Cromwell came to power it had done its work. He and his generation had been nourished from childhood on tales of the Armada and persecutions in the Netherlands. To them, Spain represented all those evils that had so alarmed the Puritans of Elizabeth's reign: cruelty, immorality, and religious oppression. By the standards of his day, Cromwell was a remarkably tolerant man, but this toleration did not extend to Roman Catholics. These he hated with an unbalanced passion, and his view of Spain and its Church was not unlike a Spanish crusader's attitude toward the Grand Turk. When the government of England fell into the hands of this domineering and self-confident man, a revival of Elizabethan anti-Hispanism was inevitable.

The marvel is that it came so late. When Cromwell strode into the House of Commons on April 20, 1653, and summarily dismissed the Rump, England was engaged in a fratricidal struggle with the Netherlands over a variety of issues, most of which were concerned with trading and fishing rights. After the defeat and death of Admiral Tromp in the summer of that same year the Dutch began to seek a peaceful settlement, leaving Cromwell free to concentrate on the

Catholic powers. His first interest at this point was to strike a blow on behalf of the French Huguenots, and to this end he actually considered making a treaty of alliance with Spain! His purpose in doing this was obvious. Like many Englishmen, he was certain that the possession of the American mines gave Spain an almost unlimited supply of bullion. In essence, then, he was blackmailing Cardenas, the Spanish ambassador, into advancing him money for a war with France.[1] In this case his tactics failed. The Spaniards had no money to spare and were unwilling to grant him free access to the West Indies as the only other acceptable price of alliance. Suddenly perceiving that the Huguenots were in no real danger, Cromwell prepared to turn on Spain.

Somehow, one is inclined to agree with Gardiner that the whole episode presents "at best, a sorry spectacle."[2] Long before the negotiations had broken down, Cromwell was already plotting seriously against his unsuspecting would-be allies. The story of the "Western Design," as it came to be known, is worth telling here, for in it all the signal elements of anti-Hispanism are present: its influence on statecraft and its regrettable tendency to turn back and feed upon itself in an unending cycle of hatred and prejudice. Our tale begins at a meeting of the Protector's Council, April 20, 1654.

According to Edward Montagu's notes, the discussion was opened by Cromwell himself, who remarked that on conclusion of the Dutch Peace England's fleet of 160 vessels had been left idle and that 30 of them, through some providential coincidence, were already in the West Indies. Obviously, they would have to be employed somewhere, and it was Cromwell's opinion that they might better be used against Spain than France. Attacking France might prove hazardous, and it would certainly be unprofitable in a financial sense. Then, too, Spain was more anti-Protestant and therefore more deserving of chastisement.[3] The Protector was apparently musing out loud, but when objections were raised his mood seemed to intensify. When asked about the loss of the Spanish trade, the possible closure of Gibraltar, and the commercial advantage that would undoubtedly accrue to the Dutch, his answer was simple and characteristic: "God will provide."[4]

Though negotiations with Spain were still in progress, it must have been abundantly clear to his intimates that they were destined to failure. Two months later, Cromwell presented his plan in greater detail to the members of his Council, and the "Western Design" was launched. The exchange that took place on that occasion is noteworthy as evidence of how far Cromwell was indebted to the Elizabethans, for Lambert, alone among the members of his Council, questioned the wisdom of his proceeding. With remarkable foresight, Lambert declared that an attack on the Indies would be expensive, difficult, and unprofitable to Protestantism. Cromwell's reply, thought not strictly relevant, was clear: "God hath brought us hither to consider the work that we may do in the world as well as at home."[5] He seemed to feel that the whole project could be financed by cruising the Spanish Main for prizes and that the war, like those of Elizabeth's day, would be confined to the Americas.[6] Experience was to prove him wrong on both counts, but prejudice and his own powerful will had carried him beyond the reach of argument. Though Lambert's objections were wise and even prophetic, they seemed to make no impression. On December 20, 1654, a fleet set sail for the New World under the joint command of Generals Penn and Venables.

By any reasonable standard, the expedition was a fiasco. Driven from Hispaniola by a handful of the local residents, the English moved on to Jamaica, which they were able to seize without much difficulty. For the moment, prospects seemed to improve, but Lambert's gloomiest forebodings were realized as the two generals squabbled over precedence, the troops died of fever and starvation, and the costs mounted alarmingly. All things considered, it was a most un-Cromwellian failure, worthy of the muddled thinking that had produced it.

That the West Indian expedition should ever have taken place is at least partially a credit to the strength of anti-Hispanism, not only in Cromwell himself but in the hearts of those around him. To us, the arguments advanced in Council are absurd, but with the honorable exception of Lambert no one there present seems to have opposed them. As sycophants were notoriously rare in the New Model Army, we must assume that Cromwell's feelings were shared by most of his associates. The reasons for this vehemence are best seen in the attempts made by the government to justify its undertaking.

These attempts were neither compendious nor revealing. Whether oratorical or literary, they added little of interest to the growing body of anti-Spanish polemics and, for the most part, contented themselves with reiterating the standard accusations of earlier pamphleteers and historians. Cromwell's speech to Parliament was a perfect example. As in the two Council meetings, the Protector seemed almost inarticulate with rage and hatred. The burden of his address was the essence of simplicity: "Why truly, your great Enemy is the Spaniard. He is. He is a natural enemy. He is naturally so throughout, by reason of that enmity that is in him against whatsoever is of God."[7] Making no attempt to introduce new arguments, Cromwell continually reiterated this theme, referring occasionally to "the several assassinations designed upon that Lady, that great Queen," and "the blood of your poor people unjustly shed in the West Indies."[8] That most of this blood, according to a later declaration,[9] had been shed prior to 1608 made no difference. The sins of the fathers would presumably be visited upon the sons.

The declaration referred to above was perhaps the most systematic exposition of Cromwell's views on Spain. Entitled *A Declaration of His Highnes By the Advice of His Council, Setting forth On Behalf of this Commonwealth, the Justice of their Cause against Spain*, it was not printed until early in 1655, as the expedition had sailed in what was supposed to have been secrecy. Like Cromwell's speech, it was vigorous, if not strictly logical. Its only real argument was that Spain had deprived the English of their God-given right to trade in the West Indies.[10] In support of this thesis, the anonymous author presents a list of ten ships seized by the Spaniards between 1605 and 1608, but there are no incidents of more recent date, and the details in each case are remarkably similar. The valiant English invariably fall victim to a low Spanish trick, often engineered by a priest, and are tortured to death following the seizure of their goods. The destruction of the Puritan colony at Providence Island in 1641, though more serious, is barely mentioned. In all cases, the evidence is scanty and circumstantial, but if the reader's memory were long enough it might serve to justify the conclusion that the Spaniards had "con-

tinually invaded in a hostile manner, Our Colonies, slain Our Countrymen, taken Our Ships and Goods, destroyed Our Plantations,
made Our People Prisoners and Slaves, and have continued so doing."[11] If the reader's memory did not, by any chance, extend to the
days in which this statement was true, he could always be reminded
of other, more familiar matters. After all, "God will have an account
of the Innocent Blood of so many Millions of Indians, so barbarously
butchered by the Spaniards,"[12] and the Armada "must needs lie
close by English mens hearts, and will not easily out of their
minds."[13] With commendable restraint, the author says "nothing
of the bloody Spanish Inquisition, (a common cause of quarrel to
all Protestants)."[14]

One almost feels sorry for the man whose task it was to write this
pamphlet. He must have known how thin his arguments would sound
in the unlikely event that anyone would oppose them, for he is
forced back upon the most pitiful of expedients:

> . . . the blood and spoils of our own Countrymen, being sufficient to
> warrant the late Expedition, besides the Consideration of Present Interest,
> and future Security to this Nation, and all its Allies, especially of the
> Protestant Religion, with sundry other Reasons and Motives which
> were inducements to that undertaking, the which it is not our Business
> (at present) to declare.[15]

These "Reasons and Motives" were never formally announced, but
perhaps they were comprehended in a final statement worthy of the
Protector himself: "The Glory of God and the advancement of
Christ's Kingdom will ultimately appear to be the principal end of
the expedition."[16]

The idea of a religious crusade against Spain was not new in 1655.
For nearly three generations, the more vehement English Protestants
had been calling incessantly for nothing less. Their viewpoint was
now urged with unparalleled vigor by John Milton and a number
of lesser writers. Milton, as Latin secretary to the Protector, under-
took to advance the same arguments of the *Declaration* in a Latin
Manifesto, published like its vernacular counterpart, in 1655.[17] Then
there was the curious pamphlet entitled, *A Dialogue, Containing a
Compendious Discourse concerning the Present Designe in the West*

Indies. Cast in the form of a discussion between a soldier and a Puritanical sailor, it attempts to justify the proceedings on the highest of moral grounds. The soldier is not pro-Spanish, but as an honest man he is concerned about the justice of such an apparently unprovoked attack and confides his doubts to the seaman. The answer is long and reminiscent of Cromwell's own answer to Lambert. It would seem that the war was begun because the Lord brought England from darkness into light, and scripture commands that this work should go from nation to nation.[18] The soldier admits that this is true and agrees that "darkness" is synonymous with the Pope, who must be brought low as soon as possible. When this is agreed upon, the seaman concludes as follows:

> Sir, if the Pope must fall, then the Pillars or Main Supporters on which his power standeth must first be removed: And if so, then Spain must first be aimed at, who is his Right Hand; for he, and only he, viz. the Spaniard, maintains that bloody Inquisition, that crimson Gulf, in which thousands of poor souls are (on all occasions) secretly swallowed up and sent to their Beds of Darkness.[19]

On the Continent the Thirty Years War had come to an end but seven years previously. Men still believed, as yet another writer put it, that any war is just if it opposes "Idolaters, Heretics, and Members of the false Church," but even if they were inclined to be tolerant, they should never be allowed to forget that "conquest is free to all people, no Law of Nations can prohibit the power of the Sword."[20]

The thinking mirrored in these publications was typical of Cromwell and may be taken as a fairly accurate summary of his reasons for attacking the possessions of Spain. The pamphlets and his own statements in Council indicate what might easily have been guessed: that Cromwell was familiar with anti-Spanish literature and in tune with the spirit of Foxe and Hakluyt. His actions can be explained fully in no other way. There was little to be gained from an attack on the West Indies and much to be lost, as the small success of the expedition was to prove. Anyone of Cromwell's undoubted ability would have realized this had he not been blinded by irrational hatreds and a welter of misleading information. The trouble with unfavorable national stereotypes is that they lead one to underestimate the enemy. Exposed throughout his life to the concepts of Spain as set forth in this study, he failed for once in his life to make adequate preparations for a campaign. The worst troops in his regiments were sent off to their deaths with scarcely any thought being given to the peculiar difficulties of tropical warfare. Much of the blame for this must rest upon his contempt for Spain, but even more may be reserved for the hopes aroused in him by a favorite and familiar author: Thomas Gage.

Gage, as we have seen, was the author of a book whose thesis was that the seizure of Spanish colonies would be child's play for the virtuous English. There is every reason to suppose that Cromwell had read this book, and we know that in 1654 Gage personally submitted a memorial to the Protector in which he summarized and re-stated his arguments.[21] Though biased and inaccurate, Gage's information on the West Indies was accepted without question at Whitehall.[22] In this manner, the literary anti-Hispanism once again found its way into the councils of the mighty.

If the "Western Design" was typical of the devastating effects the Black Legend might possibly have produced, it was also typical of those situations in which anti-Hispanism, having helped to produce an incident, could then renew itself by feeding upon the results. Obviously, the government's attempt to justify its policy encouraged a reawakening of hostile interest, but the resumption of open war after so many years of relative quiet produced a new rash of literature on Spain and its colonies. Only a small portion of this was devoted to current events. As in the Cadiz expedition of 1625, patriotism was forced to keep silent in the absence of victory. Some pamphlets, such as *A Brief and perfect Journal of the late Proceedings and Successe of the English Army in the West Indies*, contained little news and much exhortation to greater efforts. Another, celebrating the victory of Montague and Blake over the Spanish fleet in 1657, declared:

> When our Protector looking with disdain
> Upon the gilded majesty of Spain,
> And knowing well that Empires must decline,

Whose chief support and sinews are of Coin,
Our Nations solid virtue did oppose,
To the rich Troublers of the world's repose.[23]

But otherwise, all was silent. Dysentery and tropical fevers are not news, nor are desultory campaigns against bands of runaway Negroes, but it must be admitted that there was another reason for this unwonted restraint. A new phenomenon had arisen to plague the literate Englishman: the ancestor of the modern newspaper.

During the complex troubles of the Civil War, a shoal of tiny newsletters had emerged to resolve the confusions of the period according to the preconceptions of their editors. The most important of these was the *Publick Intelligencer*. Though by no means a major element in the Black Legend, this relatively respectable journal was always prepared to tell of the defeat of fifty Spaniards at the hands of five shipwrecked mariners,[24] or of Captain Salmon's success against two men-of-war in his merchant ship, the *Prudent Mary*.[25] Needless to say, such releases were filled with illuminating discourses on the cowardice of all Spaniards. The *Intelligencer*'s counterpart, *Mercurius Politicus*, though not so active in seeking out military news, was quick to print "a Copie of the heads of a late new ranting Edict or proclamation of the King of Spain," with appropriate comments on Spanish pride and insolence.[26] These efforts, whatever their shortcomings, are worth noting as an example of what news was available to the English public in 1655 and 1656.

In the absence of good news, it was again necessary to follow the example of one's fathers and compile catalogs of Spanish villainies—most of which had been committed beyond the reach of living memory. This task was gleefully undertaken by one J. H., author of *The King of Spains Cabinet Council Divulged; or a Discovery of the Prevarications of the Spaniards*. The result of his labors was a ponderous tome of no less than thirty chapters in which nearly every crime committed by Spaniards during the past 150 years is listed under the appropriate type of "prevarication." As a summary of the Puritan view of history it is unsurpassed, though its title is irrelevant and its organization eccentric. The "prevarications" themselves are a misnomer. Most of them actually refer to plots of one kind or another, but they also include such relatively candid affairs as the Armada and the peace treaty of 1604.[27] Their one unifying feature was that all were designed to further Spain's dream of universal monarchy and encompass the downfall of Protestantism.

As this work was admittedly a compilation from older sources, few of the tales added anything new to the legend of Spanish perfidy. An exception was the chapter entitled "The Prevarications and excesses of the Spaniards against the Kingdom or Principal of Catalonia." Of itself, the Catalonian revolt was of little interest to most Englishmen. In 1642 it had received cursory mention in a pamphlet published two years after the event,[28] but no details were printed until *The King of Spains Cabinet Council* was "divulged" in 1658. When the information did reach England, it was so stuffed with hyperbole and padded with imaginary facts that it was of no value whatever to anyone but a propagandist. Even towns mentioned as the site of some dreadful atrocity prove, on examination, to be nonexistent; but this tampering with actuality is no more fanciful than the author's ideas on the cause of the troubles. In his view, the Catalans rebelled because the Spaniards had been vexing, torturing, and oppressing them for over twenty years.[29] Even the poorest of them had been forced to quarter up to twelve soldiers at a time in their own homes, and these soldiers had done nothing but commit "adulteries, rapes, murders, plunders, house-breakings and firings" during the whole of their stay.[30] When the citizens of Perpignan complained, their city was destroyed with fire balls, their churches were pillaged, and they themselves found their arms confiscated.[31] To put it in the plainest possible terms:

> In Catalonia there is nothing seen or heard, but women bewailing the murderings of their husbands, and husbands the ravishing of their wives, and abusing of their marriage beds: old men complaining of the violating of their daughters, and the daughters lamenting the loss of their chastity: Orphans howling for the violent death of their parents, & both Citizens and Country-men invoking the help of Heaven in these calamities &c.[32]

Such a passage calls up memories of the Dutch revolt, and the present writer hereby apologizes for including another example of this turgid sensationalism. If half a century had not improved the literary quality of anti-Spanish writings, it must also be confessed that their accuracy was equally immune to progress. In this particular case, there is scarcely a word of truth in the whole account. To begin with, the unrest in Catalonia was due to a conflict between centralizing ministers in Madrid and the Catalans themselves, who jealously sought to maintain their ancient "Constitutions" intact. No troops entered the Principality until it was invaded by the French in 1639, and even then no attempt was made to quarter them on the people until it became obvious that the Catalans were unwilling to lift a finger in their own defense.[33] Quartering, it should be remembered, did not involve the actual placement of soldiers in private homes but a kind of levy for their material support, thus rendering the burden financial rather than personal. Nevertheless, the burden was a real one, and it cannot be denied that unpleasant incidents between the soldiers and their unwilling hosts took place. The Spanish troops were, as usual, ill-paid and ill-fed, and their condition was aggravated by the insults of Catalan nationalists, who did everything in their power to make an intolerable situation worse. It would not have been surprising had the wholesale attrocities mentioned by "J. H." taken place, but in actual fact the recorded instances of such behavior are few, and when they did occur Spaniards were rarely involved. As in the Netherlands, much of the blame for disorderly conduct must fall upon the large numbers of Flemish and Neapolitan mercenaries who lacked both the discipline and the incentives of their Castilian employers.[34]

Like the maltreatment of civilians, the bombardment of Perpignan unquestionably took place, but once again in circumstances quite different from those described by our author. In frightened response to an outbreak of rioting, the town council refused admittance to a group of Spanish soldiers under Geri de la Rena and called for outside help in resisting them. Starving and desperate, the Spaniards opened fire and destroyed a major part of the town before the city fathers would capitulate.[35] Subsequent relations with the townspeople were understandably strained.

The events described here had, as we have mentioned, little direct influence on England. Though important to the fortunes of Spain and France, the Catalan revolt failed to encourage much anti-Hispanism beyond the borders of Catalonia itself. The only justification for discussing this chapter at such length is to demonstrate the mendacity of its author and to show that the methods by which the Black Legend was first developed could be revived, when necessary, at a later date. Thanks to the remoteness of this ugly affair, it will always take second place in the affections of Englishmen to the trials of their close neighbors and coreligionists, the Dutch; but the historical method used in both cases is similar, and the conclusions that contemporary readers were expected to draw are the same.

As for the author, his treatment of this episode shows that he could sustain his flights of fancy beyond the mere embroidering of other men's fables. It is therefore easier to understand his conviction that Spaniards were responsible for all placards issued against heresy by Charles V,[36] and that the Spanish Inquisition had murdered no fewer than 150,000 Protestants in thirty years' time.[37] So great was his lack of good faith that he referred to Hessels, the Dutch inquisitor, as "Diego Hesselio" in the forlorn hope that unwary readers might mistake him for a Spaniard.[38] History was once again prostrating itself before the golden calf of politics.

The King of Spains Cabinet Council Divulged is propaganda on its lowest level. Its importance at this time reflects both the anxiety of Cromwell's government to justify their unprovoked attack on Spanish territory and the difficulty of finding talented spokesmen for their views. In John Milton they possessed a writer of the first magnitude, but Milton was only one very busy man. He could not be expected to represent Cromwell's case on all levels, and it was perhaps best that he be reserved for the highest level of them all: explanations in the international language of scholarship and diplomacy. When the time came to take the matter to the English people, it was found that the literary resources of the Protectorate were lacking in depth. The fortunate Elizabeth had never been faced with this difficulty, but in their hatred of frivolity the Puritans had effectively discouraged all but the most didactic and edifying of literary forms. The drama, in particular, had suffered from their displeasure, and many of the nation's writers found themselves lending comfort to the Royalists in exile. Among the beleaguered poets was Sir William D'Avenant.

The son of an Oxford vintner, D'Avenant supported the King, was knighted at the siege of Gloucester in 1643, and ultimately retired to Paris where he became a Catholic. On a mission to Virginia his ship was captured by the Parliamentarians, and it was only by the narrowest of margins that he escaped the gallows. It has been suggested that Milton intervened on his behalf,[39] but whatever the source of his good fortune, he was soon at work on two masques entitled *The Cruelty of the Spaniards in Peru* and *The History of Sir Francis Drake*. This fact is in itself extraordinary, for while Cromwell and his associates were not as dour as they are sometimes pictured, they were certainly no lovers of the theater, and this resort to a playwright must have been galling in the extreme. To be sure, *The History of Sir Francis Drake* was performed in the reign of Oliver's son, but its predecessor may well have been approved by the old Protector himself.[40]

In content, these efforts are as trivial as one might expect. As with most masques, they were intended as vehicles for music, dancing, and spectacle, entertainments roughly corresponding in their own quaint way with our musical comedies. No serious message need be expected from such a medium, but in this case at least it was definitely intended to serve a serious purpose. *The Cruelty of the Spaniards in Peru* opens with a prophetic speech delivered by the high priest of the Indians. This worthy is concerned that the Inca's prohibited love for someone other than his own sister will bring destruction in the form of "cruel men, idolators of gold," who are even now preparing to descend upon the country.[41] No sooner does he conclude than the Spaniards themselves appear and stage a rousing battle with the Indians, following which they celebrate their victory by dancing a *sarabanda*. Then:

A dolefull Pavanne is plai'd to prepare the change of the Scene which represents a dark Prison at great distance; and farther to the view are discerned Racks and other Engines of torment, with which the Spaniards are tormenting the Natives and English Mariners, which may be supposed to be lately landed there to discover the Coast. Two Spaniards are likewise discovered . . . the one turning a Spit, whilst the other is basting an Indian Prince which is roasted at an artificial fire.[42]

The high priest enters, deplores the situation in verse, and, "his speech being ended, he waves his Verge, and his Attendant performs the *Porpoise*." In the climax of this dismal scene, the Indians, fettered in silver, are driven into the woods by "an insulting Spaniard with a truncheon." After a brief interval they reappear, laden with bullion, and are forced by the Spaniard "to fall into a Halting Dance."[43]

Deliverance, however, is at hand. A troop of red-clad Englishmen and befeathered Peruvian auxilliaries are shown chasing the Spaniards, who flee in great disorder. Once again, the priest enters, praises the English, "waves his Verge, and his Attendant performs the *Double Somerset*." In his stage directions, the author admits that nothing of the kind ever happened, "but yet in Poetical Representations of this nature, it may pass as a Vision discerned by the Priest of the Sun before the matter was extant."[44] The whole program ends with a joint triumph of the English and the Indians over a "prideful and sullen" Spaniard whom they "salute with their feet."[45]

The Cruelty of the Spaniards in Peru may not have been great art, but its purpose was as plain as was its debt to Las Casas. Its successor, *The History of Sir Francis Drake*, was even more wandering and disorganized, with more modest sets and none of the unconscious humor that makes the *Spaniards in Peru* almost palatable. Based on Drake's exploits in Panama, it is chiefly concerned with the taking of Nombre de Dios and with the troubles of the Cimarrons, escaped Negro slaves who aided the English. Whatever the numerous shortcomings of this work, it makes its point clearly, though in the form of a thinly disguised parable. When Drake rebukes his wild allies for breaking up a creole wedding feast and stealing the bride, their leader pleads for them in the following terms:

> And noble Chief, the cruelties which they
> Have often felt beneath the Spaniards sway,
> (Who midst the triumphs of our Nuptial feasts
> Have forc'd our Brides & slaughter'd all our guests)

> May some excuse even from your Reason draw:
> Revenge does all the fetters break of Law.[46]

This last line may, in itself, express much of the spirit behind Cromwell's project in the West Indies. The frequent references to past atrocities indicates that revenge, together with a certain resurgence of the crusading spirit, played a considerable part in launching Penn and Venables on their ill-fated adventure. If the propaganda barrage that accompanied them seemed halfhearted at times, perhaps it was because the thirst for retribution had already been instilled in the English soul and needed only to be reawakened at leisure. Cromwell may not have sought a revival of Elizabethan foreign policy, but he certainly aroused a good deal of neo-Elizabethan sentiment.

By way of example, we may cite those works which attempted to revive the Elizabethan spirit of enterprise in the manner of Hakluyt. When arguing with his Council, Cromwell had, in effect, paraphrased the famous remark of Bernal Díaz del Castillo, who claimed that he had gone to the Indies to serve God, and also to get rich. It is doubtful that profit was the primary consideration in planning the "Western Design," but it certainly had its place. Men still ached to get their hands on the dwindling riches of Mexico and Peru, and the urge to colonize was still very much alive. Among those who sought to encourage such passions was the entrepreneur, Sir Ferdinando Gorges. As the possessor of large proprietary grants in North America, Gorges had every incentive to the further encouragement of overseas expansion and took to the pen to set forth his arguments. His *America Painted to the Life*, is a fair representation of one important form of persuasion: incitement to wrath. The argument is a familiar one. To Gorges, the Spaniards had no business in the Indies to begin with, and they forfeited such claims as they may have possessed by their Godless cruelty and failure to plant effectively the more remote areas of their empire. These contentions are supported by an equally familiar view of American history:

> Had the commanders that came afterwards been men of as much prudence and moderation as the first discoverers were, the King of Spain had certainly won him much more Repute in the Conquest of those

People . . . but so greedy of wealth and addicted to rapine were the Governors of Provinces themselves, so little did they execute those Acts of Grace which were granted to the Indians by the King, and Council for Indian Affairs, so far did they indulge to the barbarous license of Soldiers, that whosoever shall read the historical, admirable, and true Account of their cruel Massacres and Slaughters of above Twenty millions of innocent people, in a Treatise Entitled, *The Tears of the Indians*, to be sold by him that prints this Volume, I say, whosoever shall read that bloody Treatise, the very name of a Spaniard will be hateful to him.[47]

That "bloody Treatise" was, of course, the *Brevissima Relación*, reissued for the benefit of a new generation that might somehow have neglected the original.

The high moral tone of Gorges's arguments was perhaps a necessity, as it had been in the days when Hakluyt was compiling his magnificent work on much the same subject. It is a credit to mankind that even our most outrageous burglaries are accompanied by deep searchings of the mind and heart. But before the would-be burglar can examine his motives, he must have some foreknowledge as to the nature of the prospective loot. This was provided, in Cromwell's day, by a gentleman known to us only as "N. N." His *America: or An exact Description of the West-Indies* is a latter-day counterpart of those lists of trade goods and natural resources that make some sections of Hakluyt virtually unreadable. Dedicated to the London merchant, John Robinson, it is the type of book that would appeal to an astute businessman bent on making his profit from the new switch in foreign policy. As a result, contributions to anti-Hispanism are made strictly in passing. We are told, for example, that at Potosí the Indians work day and night without rest and that many of them are horribly maimed by accidents under ground.[48] The Spaniards are blamed for introducing venereal disease into Europe,[49] and the massacre of the French colony in Florida is recounted at some length.[50] In all fairness, though, such outbreaks of feeling are rare. *America: or An exact Description of the West-Indies* is a cool and calculated look at the condition of someone else's property. The Black Legend had come full circle.

CHAPTER X. CONCLUSION

In the year 1660, a pamphlet appeared in London titled *The Character of Spain: Or, An Epitome of Their Virtues and Vices*. It is an unremarkable work, neither better nor worse than its many predecessors, but its declared purpose and the time at which it appeared make it a fitting climax to this study. 1660 was, of course, the year of the Restoration. Oliver Cromwell was dead, and his son Richard had retired to congenial obscurity after a brief and uninspiring term as Lord Protector. The new king, Charles II, was far too sophisticated, and perhaps too sympathetic to Catholicism, to seek a continuation of Cromwell's policies. For the moment, at any rate, Elizabethan adventuring was once more in eclipse.

This is an important point to remember, for *The Character of Spain*, like Wordsworth's idea of poetry, was intended to represent emotion recollected in tranquillity. Virtually unconnected with the shifting requirements of international politics, and written at a time when most Englishmen were concerned with business of a far more pressing nature, this portrait of a nation may be taken as a fair example of what the English thought of their venerable enemy after a century of intermittent warfare.

Unlike most of the works that preceded it, this pamphlet acknowledges little debt to history. It was one of three "Epitomes" that sought to delineate the national characteristics of the French, the Italians, and the Spaniards, without dabbling in the mundane waters of substantiation. Historical anecdotes are used sparingly, and while none of the portraits is flattering, the Spaniards are made to appear particularly reprehensible.

The author begins with a decription of the country itself. To him, "Tis Nature's Sweating-tub, a Nest of Wolves, the very seat of Hunger and Famine." No one "was ever prompted by his fancy to a second visit."[1] The inhabitants of this earthly inferno are about what one might expect them to be. They are so tightfisted that they learned geometry to measure the circumference of their bread,[2] and so ambitious that "they are the very Harpies of the earth."[3] "Pride, haughtiness, and Ambition, accompanied with an imaginary conceit of their own peculiar *Grandeza*, are the Ingredients that usually go to the composition of a Spaniard."[4] So great is their ostentation that none of them will engage in crafts, and even the lowliest beggars discourse on their noble birth, concocting ingenious stories to account for their present low estate. Worst of all, some of them seem to think themselves as good as the king![5] To a class-ridden Englishman, fresh from the chilly mists and riotous vegetation of his native island, such impressions were not unnatural, but the notions of Spanish cruelty and treachery came not from personal experience but from Las Casas. Overcoming his usual aversion to scholarly references of any kind, the author informed his readers that "as to their [the Spaniards'] cruelty, it was so inhuman that the relation thereof would stagger the belief of a Christian, were there not a general consent among Historiographers of the heinousness thereof."[6] If the meager evidence given in support of this statement is an indication, "Historiographers" refers exclusively to the worthy Bishop of Chiapas; but by 1660 the quality of one's citations was even less important than it had been in 1588. The author was telling his readers what they already knew, and the millions of dead Indians required no more documentation than did the tyrannies of Alba or the instruments of torture in the ships of the Armada. In short, he could conclude without fear of contradiction that "tis impossible that so much villainy as hath been acted by that Nation should be forever unpunished."[7]

By now these phrases have the leaden ring of familiarity. The literature of anti-Hispanism is nothing if not redundant, and the hoary generalizations contained in The Character of Spain are as typical as they are comprehensive. A coherent if unfavorable and highly colored picture of Spain had emerged from the welter of invective, and there is every reason to believe that it was accepted by a large portion of contemporary English society. As seen in this pamphlet of 1660, the components of the picture were greed and immorality, cruelty, treachery, and overweening pride. The only serious omission was that, unlike many of his predecessors, our writer refused to tax the enemy with cowardice in battle. In this he was wise, for of all the charges brought against the Spaniards, this was the least defensible. Whatever else they may have done, Spanish soldiers rarely ran from a fight.

A far more curious omission, from the modern point of view, is the complete indifference shown, not only in this pamphlet but throughout the literature of the entire period, to Spain's intellectual achievements or the lack of them. It will be remembered that Juderías and the Hispanists were primarily angered by the legend of Spanish backwardness and ignorance, but here, in the sixteenth and seventeenth centuries, only Thomas Gage attempted to raise the point, and then only with regard to Spanish America. What accounts for this strange lapse? Surely, had it occurred to them, the English propagandists would have used this weapon as readily as any other, but for some reason they did not do so. That dubious pleasure was reserved for the great French writers of the eighteenth century, whose hatred for Catholic thought was certainly no greater than that of John Foxe. It would be tempting to say that the late flowering of this particular myth was an honest reflection of Spain's declining intellectual eminence, but the fact that such eminence would scarcely have been recognized by Protestants and freethinkers at any time and the blatant exaggerations of Spain's insularity that were accepted at face value by the philosophes indicate that we must seek our answer elsewhere. Perhaps the most reasonable explanation is that there was a change in the anti-Spanish writers themselves. In the sixteenth century the men who wrote against Spain were, for the most part, neither scholars nor intellectuals. To them, such standards of comparison would have seemed quite irrelevant. English anti-Hispanism was originally founded on moral rather than intellectual grounds and in its first phase was based on a concept of inherent Spanish wickedness. Only the proponents of a self-conscious intellectualism could declare that Africa began at the Pyrenees.

Tracing the evolution of this early form of anti-Hispanism has been the primary purpose of this study. From what we have seen, it is evident that it sprang from historical causes in the widest sense of the term, and that it developed in close harmony with subsequent historical events. Like most widely held notions, it succeeded in taking root because the ground had been well-prepared by developments of a more general nature. The first and most important of these was the Reformation. Many, if not all, of the writers who contributed to the Black Legend were staunch, even fanatical Protestants. Their hatred for Spain was based on such essentially religious issues as the treatment of Protestants by the Inquisition and the persecutions in the Netherlands. Even the formal content of anti-Spanish literature, its scriptural imagery and wealth of biblical citations, reflects the enormous influence of Protestant feeling. On another level, it is quite likely that Spain's most offensive acts were themselves inspired by motives of a partially religious nature, and had there been no conscious attempt to destroy the work of the Reformation there would have been little cause for righteous indignation. Had there been no such deep religious antagonism, English and, indeed, European attitudes toward Spain would certainly have been quite different.

The baleful influence of national consciousness is not so easy to assess. Englishmen were unquestionably aware of their national identity, and such writers as Raleigh, Thomas Scott, and Sir Richard Hawkins took great delight in comparing England's virtues with the vices of its perfidious enemy. The frequent insistence on the supposed Moorish or Jewish origins of the Spaniards indicates that there may even have been an element of racial antagonism involved, but how important could such a thing have been? Few Englishmen of the sixteenth or seventeenth century would ever have seen a Spaniard face to face, a fact which certainly militated against the development of deep personal hatreds as much as it inhibited mutual understanding. Contrary to modern mythology, extensive contact between different ethnic groups does not invariably produce love and respect; but in this case, at any rate, the opportunity to develop truly Balkan hatreds was generally lacking. Though the Englishmen of the Tudor and Early Stuart period were well aware of their own unique nationality, and equally conscious of the pure strangeness of others, their feelings had not yet developed into true nationalism or racism as we understand it today. In general, their attitude was far more naive, and at the same time more practical.

It must be remembered that when Elizabeth I came to the throne, the whole idea of nationality was a relatively new one. War and politics had, time out of mind, been involved with dynastic or, at best, religious questions. The Hundred Years War and other such adventures had permitted Englishmen to discover that they were unlike other men, but they were not yet sure how this happened to be, or why. Natural curiosity encouraged them to investigate the matter in a long series of books and pamphlets, some of which, like *The Character of Spain*, were devoted to nothing less than the creation of a simple national stereotype. We have already noted that such a process is perfectly natural when people are faced with a highly complex phenomenon, and it should be equally clear that Spain's misfortune lay in offending a great many nations at a time when such stereotypes were being developed all over Europe.

Moreover, the reason Spain's activities were so universally offensive at this time is in itself related to the question of national consciousness. The development of national stereotypes implies a standard of comparison with one's own nation, and in practice such comparisons were usually invidious. For a nation conscious of its own worth to behold the exaltation of a presumably inferior rival is wormwood and gall, and Spanish power was nothing if not exalted in the sixteenth century. The realization that national, rather than purely dynastic interests were involved in international struggles, may well have encouraged popular interest in issues which had hitherto been the concern of a tiny minority. It is entirely possible that many Europeans, and Englishmen in particular, felt far more closely involved in affairs of state than they had ever felt before. Thus the development of national consciousness not only contributed to the growth of anti-Hispanism but ensured its survival in an unusually malignant form.

Religious antagonisms and national consciousness, however important as conditions under which anti-Spanish feeling was allowed to mature, cannot, of course, be regarded as the immediate causes of this prejudice in England. Anti-Hispanism was directly aroused by Anglo-Spanish conflicts culminating in the Armada, and these need no further comment here. What has not been discussed is the thorny question whether or not these grievances could possibly justify such bitterness. Though personal judgments are out of place, it is hard to see how any of these events, had they been accurately reported, could possibly have done so. Many of Spain's deeds were appalling, but there is no reason to suppose that they were worse than those of any other nation. Furthermore, no complemental Anglophobia seems to have developed in Spain, where the reporting was much more subdued, though surely the Spaniards had every reason to be as vexed with the English as the English were with them. We may only conclude that much of Spain's guilt lay in the preconceptions of its self-appointed judges and that biased reporting had an enormous effect on the content of the English Black Legend.

Having said this, we are still faced with the problem of why the English fostered such grotesque exaggerations, while the Spaniards, as a rule, did not. There can be no really conclusive answer to such a question, but perhaps it has something to do with the differing internal conditions of the two countries. Spain, for once in its long and troubled history, was relatively free from religious or ideological squabbles, while its rival possessed a large Catholic minority, an enthusiastic community of more or less violent Puritans, and a great mass of citizens whose beliefs ranged from staunch Anglicanism to complete indifference. It would be easy to exaggerate the crusading fervor of the Spaniard, but he rarely had any doubts about the nature of the true Faith or who were its enemies. In all probability, he had little interest in the racial background or moral character of Englishmen. They were heretics, and it was plainly the duty of a Christian to oppose heresy wherever it might be found. For him it was just as unnecessary to hate the English because they were English as it was to hate the Moors because their skins were dark. His prejudices were based on religion and needed little fortification from the popular press.

The interested Englishman, on the other hand, was apt to find himself as one of a small group dedicated to the establishment of some particular policy, religious or otherwise. Only in times of great national crises could he count on the support of anything like the majority of his countrymen, and he was consequently obliged to spend a good deal of time in argument. If, like most of our writers, he was a Protestant of Puritanical leanings, he was apt to feel that the majority of Englishmen were in need of exhortation. Their lukewarm support for Protestant causes was reprehensible, and he could not rest until they—Catholics, Anglicans, and heathens alike—had been brought to an edifying state of hatred for the "Romish Babylon and Spanish Periander." If this could not be achieved through Godly discourse, then perhaps the reprobate could be deceived into serving God by playing upon his insular prejudices. Not all Englishmen could be counted upon to oppose Spain because that nation was inhabited by Roman Catholics, or because such opposition might bring profit to the merchants. Written propaganda was deemed necessary, and once committed to paper it was available for reference long after the Spaniards had forgotten their own more oral indignation.

This is not to suggest that our writers were invariably using dubious means in the service of a dubious cause. Those who may be called propagandists, if by propagandist we mean one who consciously attempts to influence the thoughts and behavior of others with regard to public issues, were alerting England to a very real danger. Spain was a menace, and it was well that Englishmen should have been aware of it. Whatever the individual lies and exaggerations found in these works, they were correct in their basic assumption that Spain and England were destined to be enemies until one or the other fell from its position of international influence. The tragedy came when these colorful efforts to arouse a sleeping people were accepted as reliable history by men whose literary talents, however great, did not seem to include that of critical intelligence. Exaggerations are inevitable in the heat of controversy, but there is no need to perpetuate them in the chronicles of a later day. The only possible excuse for such a lapse in judgment is that this particular "crisis" lasted, in one form or another, for over two hundred years.

With some notable exceptions, the interested persons responsible for this propaganda preferred to remain anonymous, and even when they did not, they rarely named their associates or paymasters. As one might expect, their dedications are generally addressed to the patronage of great men with Puritan leanings, but not all of the writers were interested in the same things. Some, like John Foxe, were unquestionably seeking the advancement of Protestantism, but others were merely writing in support of government policy or in encouragement of overseas enterprise. As all three of these causes involved opposition to Spain, and as many found themselves supporting all of them at once, such dividing lines are necessarily vague; but they are enough to indicate that there was not, in all probability, a single organized conspiracy to defame the Spaniards. Anti-Spanish feeling in England was aroused by a number of men, writing more or less independently and taking their examples, however inaccurate, from historical events. This feeling became a "Black Legend" only when later authors accepted their polemics as fact.

The success of this propaganda is indicated by popular opposition to the pro-Spanish policies of James I and the curious episode of Cromwell's Western Design. Neither of these developments should be taken as proof that anti-Hispanism was a ruling passion on all levels of English society, but they are examples of how a popular prejudice can influence events. Within the restricted compass of a single century, we have seen such a prejudice arise and affect international affairs in such a way as to ensure its own continuation. Many will no doubt refuse to believe that the anti-Hispanism of Cromwell and his associates played more than a very minor role in their decision to attack Spain's West Indian colonies. They will raise the specter of economic causation and attempt to justify the expedition in terms of Jamaica's annual production of "hog's butter" or the hypothetical looting of hypothetical Spanish ships; but in the end, they will be forced to admit that never was there so much hazarded in the expectation of so little gain, whether their terms of reference be political or economic. Anti-Spanish feeling in England was, and is, very real, and it has made some very real contributions to English policy.

If this is true, and the War of Jenkins's Ear no less than the interminable conflict over Gibraltar assures us that it is, why did the English not conceive a similar dislike for other nations? The various conflicts with France were more numerous and lasted every bit as long, yet the Englishman's feelings toward the French, while not always generous, do not constitute a Black Legend. One possible explanation, a favorite among the Hispanists, is that no other nation, with the possible exception of the United States, has done so much to encourage its critics. During the sixteenth and seventeenth centuries, innumerable Spaniards took to their pens in opposition to a wide range of Spanish institutions and policies. As we have seen, these writings had a tendency to fall into the hands of those who were willing to use them for their own ends. But there is another, more compelling reason. Quite simply, Englishmen rarely had an opportunity to discover that their notions of Spain and the Spaniards were erroneous. Many a young man set out on a Grand Tour, but such tours did not as a rule include a visit to Spain. It was thought to be a poor place, located far from the highroad of European culture, which, as everyone knew, extended in a direct line from London through Paris to Rome. As a result, while English gentlemen were able to form an intimate acquaintance with France and Italy, they remained dependent upon the information of others for their knowledge of Spain. With too few exceptions, this information came from the sources we have been examining.

There is also the fact, which cannot be overemphasized, that England was but one of a number of nations whose experience with Spain had been unpleasant. No great empire, whatever its policies, can avoid incurring the wrath of its neighbors; and the wide range of Spanish activities, not only against England but in the Netherlands, France, and Italy, left Spain peculiarly vulnerable to hostile criticism. At least three other countries had developed their own Black Legends in a manner not unlike that of England. When the honest Englishman turned to his neighbors for enlightenment, he found his worst suspicions confirmed and the prejudice of his countrymen justified. For all their differences, England's cultural ties with France and the Netherlands have always been close, and their separate strains of anti-Hispanism tended inevitably to reinforce each other. It was in this way that the legend of Spanish barbarism was allowed to grow and to become part of the intellectual baggage of Western man. Though a product of history, it had no basis in fact. Though patently unfair, it continues to color our view of an entire culture. At this moment, anti-Hispanism may well be in the process of being supplanted by anti-Americanism, but this fact does not make it less worthy of our attention.

NOTES

CHAPTER I. INTRODUCTION

1. Julián Juderías, *La Leyenda Negra*, 4th ed. (Barcelona, 1917), p. 20.
2. Ibid., p. 266.
3. Ibid., p. 309.
4. Ibid., p. 315.
5. Ibid., pp. 339–341.
6. Sverker Arnoldsson, *La Leyenda Negra: Estudios sobre sus orígenes* (Göteborg, 1960), pp. 12–13.
7. Ibid., p. 14.
8. Ibid., p. 105.
9. Such works as C. S. Forester's *Hornblower* cycle and the older *Lysbeth: A Tale of the Dutch* by H. Rider Haggard come readily to mind.
10. Examples of anti-Spanish feeling in modern English writing are too numerous to list here, but a comparison of the attitudes expressed in such works as Honor Tracy's *Silk Hats and No Breakfast* (London, 1957) with those in *The Character of Spain: Or, An Epitome of Their Virtues and Vices* (London, 1660) might prove instructive.
11. Henry F. Groff and John A. Krout, *The Adventure of the American People* (New York, 1961), p. 17.
12. Ibid., pp. 19–20.
13. Melvin Schwartz and John O'Connor, *Exploring American History* (New York, 1963), p. 16.
14. Harold H. Eibling, Fred M. King, and James Harlow, *Our United States: A Bulwark of Freedom* (River Forest, Ill., 1962), p. 66.
15. Sverker Arnoldsson, *La Conquista Española de América, según la juicio de la posteridad: Vestigios de la Leyenda Negra* (Madrid, 1960), p. 24.
16. *The Prince*, chap. 21. This work was first published in England as *Il Principe de Nicolo Machiavelli . . . Con Alcune altre operette* (London, 1584).
17. Francesco Guicciardini, *The Historie of Guicciardin, conteining the warres of Italy*, trans. Geoffrey Fenton (London, 1599), p. 323.
18. Ibid., p. 1062.

CHAPTER II. THE TEARS OF THE INDIANS

1. Lewis Hanke, *Bartolomé de Las Casas: An Interpretation of His Life and Writings* (The Hague, 1951), p. 57.
2. Cédula of December 20, 1503, Isabella to Ovando, as quoted in Leslie Byrd Simpson, *The Encomienda in New Spain*, rev. ed. (Berkeley, 1950), p. 13.
3. Ibid., p. viii. For a thorough discussion of this point see R. S. Chamberlain, *Castilian Backgrounds of the Repartimiento-Encomienda*, Carnegie Institution Publications, no. 509 (Washington, D.C., 1939), pp. 15–66.
4. The sections of this document which pertain to the treatment of Indians are reprinted in Simpson, pp. 129–132.
5. Bartolomé de Las Casas, *The Spanish Colonie, or Brief Chronicle of the Actes and Gestes of the Spaniards in the West Indies, called the New World for the Space of xl. yeares* (London, 1583), p. 2.

6. Ibid., p. 1.
7. Ibid., p. 6. In this, as is all other quotations from sixteenth-century English sources, the spellings have been modernized in the interest of clarity. Grammar and punctuation have been retained as in the original.
8. Ibid., p. 48.   9. Ibid., p. 29.
10. Francisco López de Gómara, *The Pleasant Historie of the Conquest of the VVest India, now called New Spayne, atchiued by the vvorthy Prince Hernando Cortes Marquess of the valley of Huaxacas, most delectable to read* (London, 1578), pp. 152–158.
11. Bernal Díaz del Castillo, *Historia verdadera de la Conquista de la Nueva España* (Madrid, 1933), I, 266–267.
12. Las Casas, p. 40.
13. This is true even if one accepts the population estimates given by Woodrow W. Borah and S. F. Cook, *The Aboriginal Population of Central Mexico on the Eve of the Spanish Conquest* (Berkeley, 1963), p. 88.
14. Las Casas, p. 15.
15. Ibid., p. 100.   16. Ibid., pp. 40–41.
17. Sir Arthur Helps, *The Life of Las Casas, "The Apostle of the Indies"* (London, 1868), p. 6.
18. Lewis Hanke, *Bartolomé de Las Casas, Historian* (Gainesville, Fla., 1952), p. 8.
19. Las Casas, p. 6.   20. Gómara, p. 5.
21. *Dictionary of National Biography*, XIV, 432.
22. Gómara, p. 40.
23. Augustín de Zárate, *The Strange and Delectable History of the discouerie and Conquest of the Provinces of Peru in the South Sea* (London, 1581), f. 8.
24. Ibid., f. 42.
25. Ibid., f. 54.   28. Ibid., f. 65.
26. Ibid., f. 72.   29. Ibid., f. 36.
27. Ibid., f. 60.   30. Ibid., f. 59.
31. Peter Martyr d' Anghiera, *The Decades of the Newe Worlde, or West India conteyning the navigations and conquestes of the Spaniards*, trans. Richard Eden (London, 1555), p. 49.
32. Ibid., p. 55.   36. Ibid., p. 91.
33. Ibid., p. 50.   37. Ibid., p. 79.
34. Ibid., p. 107.   38. Ibid., p. 135.
35. Ibid., p. 86.   39. Ibid., p. 138.
40. Samuel Purchas, *Hakluytus Posthumus, or Purchas His Pilgrims* (Glasgow, 1902), XVII, 407.
41. Ibid., pp. 408–409.
42. Ibid., pp. 410–411.   45. Ibid., p. 299.
43. Ibid., pp. 259–260.   46. Ibid., p. 300.
44. Ibid., p. 260.   47. Ibid., p. 299.
48. José de Acosta, *The Natural and Moral History of the Indies*, trans. Edward Grimston (London, 1880). This translation was first published in 1601.

CHAPTER III. A DARK POPISH DOMDANIEL

1. John Bradford, *The Copye of a Letter, sent by John Bradforth to the right honorable lordes the Erles of Arundel, Darbie, Shrewsburye, and Pembroke, declaring the nature of the Spaniardes, and discovering the most detestable treasons which thei have pretended moste falselye agaynste our moste noble kingdome of Englande* (n.p., n.d.).

2. In Richard Hakluyt, *The Principle Voyages, Traffiques & Discoveries of the English Nation* (Glasgow, 1904), VIII, 51.

3. James Wadsworth, *The English-Spanish Pilgrime or, a New Discoverie of Spanish Popery and Iesuitical Stratagems* (London, 1630), p. 81.

4. Francis Fletcher, *The World Emcompassed by Sir Francis Drake* (London, 1628), in *Hakluyt Society*, Ser. 1, no. 16, 1854, p. 109.

5. Hakluyt, *Principle Voyages*, X, 463.

6. Henry Charles Lea, *A History of the Inquisition of Spain* (New York, 1922), III, 3.

7. Among other sources taking this view are: *A Tragicall History of the troubles and Civile warres of the lowe Countries, otherwise called Flanders* (London, 1583), I, p. 2 (hereafter cited as *A Tragicall History*); *An Historical Discourse, or rather a Tragicall History of the citie of Antwerpe* (London, 1586), p. Ai; Emanuel van Meteren, *A True Discourse Historicall of the succeeding governours in the Netherlands and the ciuill warres there begun in the yeere 1565*, trans. Thomas Churchyard and Richard Robinson (London, 1602), p. 4; and Sir Thomas Overbury, *Sir Thomas Overbury, His Observations in his Travels, Upon the State of the Seventeen Provinces, as they stood anno domini, 1609* (London, 1626), in C. H. Firth, ed., *Stuart Tracts*, pp. 213–224. Camden himself adopted this view in *The History of the Most Renowned and Victorious Princess Elizabeth, Late Queen of England*, 4th ed. (London, 1688), p. 120.

8. Quoted in M. Dierickx, "La politique religieuse de Philippe II dans les anciens Pays-bas," *Hispania*, XVI (1956), 137.

9. Ernst Schäfer, *Beiträge zur Geschichte des spanischen Protestantismus und der Inquisition* (Gütersloh, 1902), I, 22.

10. Marcel Bataillon, *Erasmo y España*, trans. Antonio Alatorre (Mexico, 1950), II, 115.

11. Ibid., p. 111.

12. Reginaldus Gonsalvius Montanus, *A Discovery and playne Declaration of sundry subtill practises of the Holy Inquisition of Spain* (London, 1568), p. Aii.

13. After publishing two preliminary and incomplete versions on the Continent in 1554 and 1559, Foxe expanded his work for the editions of 1563 and 1570. Other genuine editions appeared in 1576, 1583, 1596, 1610, 1631–1632, 1641, 1684, 1837, 1843–1849, 1870, and 1877. Bowdlerized and generally sensational editions began appearing in 1732 and have been produced with amazing regularity right down to 1954. The number of these defies cataloging here.

14. Montanus, p. Aiii.
15. *A Tragicall History*, II, 44.   16. Montanus, p. Bii.
17. R. Trevor-Davies, *The Golden Century of Spain* (New York, 1931), p. 145.
18. Henry Charles Lea, *The Inquisition in the Spanish Dependencies* (New York, 1907), pp. 391–392.
19. Montanus, p. Biii.
20. John Foxe, *Acts and Monuments,* ed. Stephen Reed Cattley (London, 1839), IV, 451.
21. Lea, *A History of the Inquisition of Spain,* I, 538.
22. Foxe, VIII, 513.
23. Ibid., p. 514.   24. Ibid., p. 516; Montanus, p. 60.
25. Hakluyt, Principle Voyages, VII, 52.
26. Montanus, p. 54.
27. Foxe, IV, 450.   28. Ibid., p. 451.
29. William Warner, *Albion's England* (London, 1602), p. 230.
30. Montanus, pp. 1–3.
31. Ibid., pp. 6–16.   33. Montanus, p. 13.
32. Foxe, IV, 451–452.   34. Ibid., p. 16.
35. John Lynch, *Spain under the Habsburgs* (Oxford, 1964), I, 25.
36. Montanus, pp. 16–17.
37. Foxe, IV, 452.   38. Montanus, p. 36.
39. Lea, *A History of the Inquisition of Spain,* III, 509.
40. Montanus, p. 22.   41. Foxe, IV, 452.
42. Lea, *A History of the Inquisition of Spain,* III, 2.
43. Ibid., pp. 18–21.
44. Ibid., p. 22.   45. Montanus, p. 27.
46. Quoted in Lea, *A History of the Inquisition of Spain,* III, 3.
47. See Montanus, pp. 23–26, and *A Tragicall History*, II, 46–47.
48. Montanus, p. Aii.   49. Ibid., p. 47.
50. *Strange and Wonderful Things happened to Richard Hasleton . . .* (London, 1595), in Edward Arber, *An English Garner* (Westminster, 1903), II, 168.
51. Hakluyt, *Principle Voyages,* IX, 428.
52. Foxe, VI, 280.
53. Lea, *A History of the Inquisition of Spain,* III, 100.
54. The exception being the pressing of those who refused to plead.
55. Conyers Read feels that this pamphlet was actually written by Thomas Norton, an associate of Walsingham and Burghley. Owing to similarities in style between it and some of Burghley's established work, I incline to the earlier view that it was indeed Burghley's own. In any event, the work was prepared at his instruction. See "William Cecil and Elizabethan Public Relations," *Elizabethan Government and Society: Essays presented to Sir John Neale,* ed. S. T. Bindoff, J. Hurstfield, and C. H. Williams (London, 1961), p. 37.
56. William Cecil, Lord Burghley, *A Declaration of the favourable dealing of her Majestie's commissioners, appointed for the examination of certayne*

traytors, and of tortures unjustly reported to be done upon them for matter of religion (1583), in *Somers Tracts*, 2nd ed. (1809), I, 212.

57. Ibid. See also *Acts of the Privy Council of England*, new series, ed. J. R. Dasent (London, 1890), VII, 373; X, 373; XIII, 37, 172, 249; XVI, 273; XVII, 310; XVIII, 63, 387; XIX, 70; XXI, 300; XXII, 40, 42, 512; XXIII, 340; XXIV, 222; XXVI, 10, 325, 373, 457, for instances of the use of torture in dealing with Catholic prisoners.

58. Cecil, *A Declaration of the favourable dealing of her Majestie's commissioners*, p. 212.

59. Ibid., 210.

60. A. O. Meyer, *England and the Catholic Church under Elizabeth*, trans. J. R. McKee (London, 1916), pp. 182–183.

61. G. B., *A Fig for the Spaniard* (London, 1591), p. 64.

62. Samuel Clark, *England's Remembrancer* (London, 1657), in *Smeeton's Historical and Biographical Tracts* (Westminster, 1819), I, 34–35.

CHAPTER IV. THE REVOLT OF THE NETHERLANDS

1. [Jacobus Verheiden], *An Oration or Speech appropriated unto the most mightie and illustrious Princes of Christendom wherein the Right and Lawfulness of the Netherlandish Warre against Phillip King of Spain is approved and demonstrated*, trans. Thomas Wood (n.p., 1624), p. 6

2. Sir Roger Williams, *The Actions of the Low Countries* (Ithaca, N.Y., 1964), p. 9. First printed London, 1618.

3. See John Lynch, *Spain under the Habsburgs* (Oxford, 1964), I, 273–275.

4. *An Historicall Discourse, or rather a Tragicall Historie of the citie of Antwerpe* (London, 1586), f. A2.

5. Verheiden, p. 3.

6. This device is found in *A Declaration & Publication of the Prince of Orange. Contayning the cause of his necessary defense against the Duke of Alva (20 July, 1568)* (London, n.d.), and *A supplication to the Kings Maiestie of Spayne, made by the Prince of Orange* (London, 1573). The *Apology* was not, to my knowledge, printed in English in its entirety. Parts of it are contained in *A Treatise against the Proclamation published by the King of Spayne by which he proscribed the late Prince of Orange* (Delft, 1580). The dating is obviously wrong. W. P. C. Knuttel, *Catalogus van de Pamfletten-Versameling berustende de Koninklijke Bibliothek* (The Hague, 1889), gives the date as 1581, but it does not seem to have reached England until after the Prince's death in 1584.

7. Thomas Churchyard, *A Lamentable and pitiful Description of the wofull warres in Flaunders . . .* (London, 1578), p. 35.

8. Pieter Geyl, *The Revolt of the Netherlands, 1555–1609* (London, 1958), p. 99.

9. [Thomas Scott], *A Tongue-Combat, Lately Happening betweene tvvo English Souldiers in the Tilt-boat of Gravesend* (London, 1623), p. 28. See also *The King of Spain's Cabinet Council Divulged* (London, 1658), p. 28.

10. *The Wicked Plots and Perfidious Practices of the Spaniards against the Seventeen Provinces of the Netherlands* . . . (1642), in *Harleian Miscellany*, V, 178.
11. Ibid. See also *The King of Spain's Cabinet Council Divulged*, p. 130.
12. *An Historicall Discourse*, f. Dii.   13. Ibid.
14. See A. L. E. Verheyden, *Le Conseil des Troubles: Liste des condamnes, 1567–1573* (Brussells, 1961).
15. *The Wicked Plots and Perfidious Practices of the Spaniards*, p. 174.
16. Geyl, pp. 107–108.
17. *A Briefe Chronicle, and perfect rehearsal of all the memorable actions happened not onlie in the low Countries, but also in Germany* . . . (London, 1598), f. C3.
18. *A Tragicall Historie*, II, 79.   20. Geyl, p. 133.
19. Ibid., p. 78.   21. Williams, pp. 103–104.
22. L. van der Essen, "Croisade contre les hérétiques ou guerre contre des rebelles: La psychologie des soldats et des officers espagnols de l'armée de Flandres au XVIe siecle," *Revue d' histoire ecclesiastique* LI, no. 1 (1956), 43.
23. Ibid., p. 45. Williams, pp. 64–65.
24. Geyl, pp. 127–129.   25. Ibid., p. 143.
26. Roger Bigelow Merriman, *The Rise of the Spanish Empire* (New York, 1934), IV, 103.
27. This is the estimate given by Henri Pirenne, *Histoire de Belgique* (Brussels, 1927), IV, 75. The lowest contemporary estimate is that of the *Historical Discourse . . . of the citie of Antwerpe*, which gives the figure as eight thousand (f. Eiii).
28. George Gascoigne, *The Spoil of Antwerp* . . . (London, 1576), p. 443.
29. Ibid., p. 431.
30. Ibid., p. 445.   31. Ibid., p. 440.
32. *The King of Spain's Cabinet Council Divulged*, pp. 18–19.
33. Gascoigne, p. 444.
34. See S. M. Pratt, "Antwerp and the Elizabethan Mind," *Modern Language Quarterly*, XXIV (1963), 53–60.
35. Perhaps the worst examples are to be found in *The King of Spain's Cabinet Council Divulged*, pp. 130–131.
36. *A Larum for London or the Siedge of Antwerpe* . . . (London, 1602), no pagination.
37. For examples, see *Newes from Antwerp* (London, 1580); *A Discourse of the present state of the Wars in the lowe Countries. Wherein is contayned the pitifull spoyle of Askot* (London, 1578); and *A briefe relation, of what is happened since the last of August 1598 by the coming of the Spanish campe into the Dukedom of Cleve* (London, 1599).
38. See n. 6 above.
39. *A supplication to the Kings of Maiestie of Spayne*, p. 12.
40. Ibid., p. 20.
41. *The true Report of the lamentable Death of William of Nassawe, Prince of Orange* . . . (Middelburg, 1584), in *Somers Tracts*, p. 410.
42. Geyl, p. 200.

43. J. B. Black, *The Reign of Elizabeth* (Oxford, 1959), p. 128.
44. *A Declaration of the Causes Moving the Queen of England to give aide to the Defence of the People afflicted and oppressed in the Lowe Countries, 1585* . . . (Richmond, 1585), in *Somers Tracts*, p. 412.
45. Ibid.   46. *Spectator*, nos. 269, 329.
47. Raphael Holinshed, *Chronicles of England, Scotland, and Ireland* (London, 1808), IV, 618.
48. Sir Richard Baker, *A Chronicle of the Kings of England* (London, 1679), p. 341.
49. Ibid., p. 353.
50. William Camden, *The History of the Most Renowned and Victorious Princess Elizabeth, Late Queen of England* (London, 1688), p. 320.
51. For a complete treatment of Meteren's life and work, see W. D. Verduyn, *Emanuel van Meteren* (The Hague, 1926).
52. Emanuel van Meteren, *A True Discourse Historicall of the succeeding governours in the Netherlands and the ciuill warres there begun in the yeere 1565* (London, 1602), p. 13.
53. Ibid., p. 15.
54. Ibid., p. 16.   57. Ibid., p. 20.
55. Ibid., p. 19.   58. Ibid., p. 67.
56. Ibid.   59. Ibid., p. 54.
60. *A Pageant of Spanish Humours* (London, 1599), no pagination.
61. Williams, p. 18; Churchyard, pp. 45, 54.
62. John Lothrop Motley, *The Rise of the Dutch Republic* (New York, 1855).

CHAPTER V. AS UNTO TRAITORS, ROBBERS, AND MURDERERS

1. George Bruner Parks, *Richard Hakluyt and the English Voyages* (New York, 1928), p. 32.
2. Ibid., p. 103.
3. Ibid., p. 2.   4. Ibid., p. 115.
5. Richard Hakluyt, *A Discourse concerning Western Planting* (Cambridge, 1877), p. 10.
6. Ibid., p. 53.
7. Ibid., pp. 72–77.   9. Ibid., p. 59.
8. Ibid., pp. 56–58.   10. Ibid., p. 69.
11. Richard Hakluyt, *Divers Voyages Touching the Discoverie of America and the Ilands Adiacent* (London, 1582), p. 4.
12. Rayner Unwin, *The Defeat of John Hawkins* (New York, 1960), pp. 127–128.
13. Unwin, pp. 183–184, maintains that an attempt was made to assassinate Hawkins in his cabin and that Hawkins fired the first shot of the engagement. Williamson doubts that such an attempt was made but asserts that the Spaniards began the attack. See J. A. Williamson, *John Hawkins* (Oxford, 1927), p. 191. For the Spanish records of the affair see *Spanish*

Documents concerning English Voyages to the Caribbean, ed. I. A. Wright, in *Hakluyt Society Publications*, ser. 2, no. 62, 1928, pp. 116–162.

14. Hakluyt, *Principle Voyages*, X, 64–74. Originally printed as Sir John Hawkins, *A true declaration of the troublesome voyadge of M. J. Hawkins to the parties of Guynea and the west-Indies* (London, 1569).
15. Hakluyt, *Principle Voyages*, X, 73.
16. Ibid., IX, 406–430, 452–489, contains the narratives of Phillips and Hortop, respectively. Hortop's account was published separately as: Job Hortop, *The travailes of an Englishman* (London, 1591).
17. Merriman, IV, 167.
18. Hakluyt, *Principle Voyages*, IX, 43–45.
19. Merriman, IV, 176.
20. Hakluyt, *Principle Voyages*, IX, 94.
21. Ibid., p. 109.   23. Merriman, IV, 176.
22. Ibid., p. 95.   24. Ibid., p. 175.
25. René de Laudonnière, *A notable historie containing foure voyages made by certayne French captaynes into Florida*, trans. Richard Hakluyt (London, 1587).
26. Hakluyt, *Principle Voyages*, IX, 106.
27. Ibid., p. 175.
28. Ibid., X, 109.   29. Ibid., VII, 52–53.
30. Ibid., X, 397. This pamphlet had been published separately as: Sir Walter Raleigh, *The discouerie of the large, rich, and bewtiful empire of Guiana. Performed in the year 1595, by Sir Walter Raleigh* (London, 1596).
31. Ibid., X, 157.   39. Purchas, XVII, 173–174.
32. Ibid., p. 114.   40. Camden, p. 249.
33. Ibid., p. 347.   41. Ibid., pp. 153–154.
34. Ibid., pp. 49–50.   42. Ibid., p. 255.
35. Ibid., p. 484.   43. Fletcher, p. 104.
36. Ibid., p. 412.   44. Ibid., p. 99.
37. Ibid., p. 472.   45. Ibid., p. 105.
38. Ibid., IX, 276.   46. Ibid., p. 106.

CHAPTER VI. THE ARMADA

1. Black, p. 250.
2. Thomas Nashe, *Pierce Pennilesse His Supplication to the Divell* (London, 1592), p. 46. This sentiment also formed the basis of Lyly's allegorical play *Midas* (London, 1592), in *The Complete Works of John Lyly*, ed. R. Warwick Bond (Oxford, 1902), III, 105–162. For the influence of the Armada on English drama see Richard V. Lindabury, *A Study of Patriotism in the Elizabethan Drama* (Princeton, 1931), p. 62.
3. There is a copy in Cecil's own hand in the *Lansdowne MSS*.
4. Hakluyt, *Principle Voyages*, VIII, 40.
5. *A True Discourse of the Armie which the King of Spaine caused to be assembled in the Haven of Lisbon . . .* (London, 1588), p. 11.
6. Camden, p. 411.   7. Verheiden, p. 59.

8. Hakluyt, *Principle Voyages*, IV, 207.
9. Warner, *Albion's England*, p. 225.
10. Garrett Mattingly, *The Armada* (Boston, 1959), p. 121.
11. *A True Discourse of the Armie*, p. 8.
12. Robert Greene, *The Spanish Masquerado* (London, 1589), f. C4.
13. [William Cecil, Lord Burghley], *The Copy of a Letter Sent Out of England to Don Bernardin Mendoza, Ambassador in France for the King of Spain, declaring the State of England* (London, 1588), in *Harleian Miscellany*, II, 71.
14. Greene, f. D4.   15. Nashe, p. 46.
16. *A Declaration of the Causes which mooved the Chiefe Commanders of the Navie . . . to take and arrest in the mouth of the River of Lisbone, certaine Shippes of corne and other provisions of warre bound for the said Citie* (London, 1589), p. 7.
17. Mattingly, *The Armada*, pp. 216–217.
18. Cecil, *Letter to Mendoza*, II, 71.   19. Mattingly, *The Armada*, p. 271.
20. Hakluyt, *Principle Voyages*, IV, 218.
21. Mattingly, *The Armada*, p. 310.
22. Samuel Clark, *England's Remembrancer* (London, 1657), pp. 17–18.
23. This is a major thesis of Mattingly's book and is corroborated by J. A. Williamson, *The Age of Drake* (London, 1938), p. 332. For a complete comparative description of the ships involved on either side, see Julian S. Corbett, *Drake and the Tudor Navy* (London, 1899), pp. 177–190.
24. Mattingly, *The Armada*, p. 334.
25. *Certain Advertisements out of Ireland, concerning the losses and distresses happened to the Spanish Navy upon the West Coasts of Ireland* (London, 1588), in *Harleian Miscellany*, II, 154.
26. Thomas Deloney, *A Joyful new Ballad declaring the happy obtaining of the great Galleazzo . . .* (London, 1588), in Edward Arber, *An English Garner*, p. 489.
27. Thomas Deloney, *A New Ballet of the strange and most cruel whips, which the Spaniards had prepared to whip and torment English men and women . . .* (London, 1588), in *An English Garner*, p. 500.
28. Ibid.
29. Deloney, *A New Ballet of the strange and most cruel whips*, p. 499.
30. Clark, p. 25. See also Thomas Scott, *A Postscript, or a Second Part of Robert, Earle of Essex his Ghost . . .* (n.p., 1642), in *Somers Tracts*, II, 606.
31. *A Skeltonical Salutation or Condign Congratulation and just vexation of the Spanishe Nation . . .* (London, 1589), p. 3.
32. Ibid., p. 4.   33. Ibid., p. 6.
34. Petruccio Ubaldini, *A Discourse concerning the Spanish Fleet Invading England in the year 1588 . . .* (London, 1590), in *Harleian Miscellany*, II, 154.
35. Ibid., p. 155.   36. Corbett, p. 265.
37. *The Coppie of the Anti-Spaniard made at Paris by a French man . . .* (London, 1590), pp. 3–5.
38. Ibid., p. 3.   40. Ibid., p. 33.
39. Ibid., pp. 27–28.   41. Ibid., p. 9.

42. Ibid., p.17.
43. Ibid., p. 18.   44. Ibid., p. 9.
45. Hakluyt, *Principle Voyages,* IV, 55.
46. Ibid., VII, 48–49.
47. Ibid., IV, 357.   48. Ibid., p. 256.

CHAPTER VII. TALES OF THE TRAVELERS

1. Gregorio Marañón, *Antonio Pérez* (Madrid, 1954), I, 253–273.
2. In the 1590's, Spanish grammars and dictionaries were produced by Corro, Stepney, Perceval, and Minsheu. Interest in the language centered around Oxford, where Corro, Pierre Bense, and others were engaged in tutoring. See Dale B. J. Randall, *The Golden Tapestry* (Durham, N.C., 1963), pp. 7–21.
3. The suggestion that this piece was written by José Teixeira has been effectively attacked by Gustav Ungerer, *Anglo-Spanish Relations in Tudor Literature* (Bern, 1956), pp. 95–99.
4. Antonio Pérez, *A Treatise Paraenetical, That is to say: An Exhortation* . . . (London, 1598), p. 106.
5. Ibid., p. 22.
6. Ibid., p. 24.   9. Ibid., p. 21.
7. Ibid., p. 111.   10. Merriman, IV, 568.
8. Ibid., p. 93.   11. Pérez, p. 19.
12. W. Nicols to Sir Peter Hollins (Jan. 25/Feb. 2, 1594-5?), *Historical Manuscripts Commission, Salisbury MSS,* V, 97.
13. Ungerer, pp. 102–149.
14. William Shakespeare, *Love's Labour's Lost,* act 1, sc. 1.
15. Ibid., act 5, sc. 1.   16. Ibid., act 1, sc. 1.
17. Albert J. Loomie, S. J., *The Spanish Elizabethans* (New York, 1963), p. 10.
18. *The Estate of English Fugitives under the king of Spaine and his ministers* (London, 1595), f. A4.
19. *A Discourse of the Usage of the English Fugitives by the Spaniard* (London, 1595), pp. 34–36.
20. Ibid., p. 39.   22. Ibid., p. 20.
21. Ibid., p. 13.   23. Ibid., p. 28.
24. *A Discourse of the Usage of the English Fugitives by the Spaniard,* p. 28. See also *The Estate of the English Fugitives,* f. I2.
25. *Dictionary of National Biography,* XX, 425–426.
26. James Wadsworth, *The Present Estate of Spain* (London, 1630), p. 74.
27. Ibid., p. 73.
28. Thomas Gage, *The English-American his Travail by Sea and Land: or, A New Survey of the West Indies* (London, 1648), p. 27.
29. Ibid., p. 151.   33. Ibid., p. 57.
30. Ibid., pp. 25–26.   34. Ibid., p. 60.
31. Ibid., p. 9.   35. Ibid., p. 103.
32. Ibid., p. 82.   36. Ibid., p. 145.

37. Ibid., p. 99.   38. Ibid., p. 189.
39. *The Estate of English Fugitives*, ff. P4-Q.
40. Lynch, I, 308.
41. Mary Elizabeth Brooks, *A King for Portugal* (Madison, Wis., 1964), pp. 48–49.
42. [José Teixeira], *The True History of the late and lamentable adventures of Don Sebastian, King of Portugal* . . . (London, 1602), in *Harleian Miscellany*, II, 358.
43. [José Teixeira], *A Continuation of the lamentable and admirable adventures of Don Sebastian, King of Portugal* . . . (London, 1603), in *Harleian Miscellany*, II, 383.
44. *Calendar of State Papers, Spanish, 1587–1603*, IV, 513.
45. [José Teixeira], *The Strangest Adventure that ever happened: either in the ages passed or present* (London, 1601).
46. Teixeira, *A True History*, II, 255–257.
47. Teixeira, *A Continuation*, II, 383.
48. *Calendar of State Papers, Spanish, 1587–1603*, IV, 273–274.

CHAPTER VIII. DIATRIBES UPON EMERGENT OCCASIONS

1. D. H. Willson, *King James VI and I* (London, 1956), pp. 271–273.
2. S. R. Gardiner, *History of England from the Accession of James I to the Outbreak of the Civil War* (London, 1896), I, 214.
3. Godfrey Davies, *The Early Stuarts, 1603–1660* (Oxford, 1959), p. 48.
4. Robert Treswell, *A Relation of such Things as were observed to happen in the Journey of the Right Honorable Charles, Earl of Nottingham, Lord High Admiral of England, his Majestys Ambassador to the King of Spain* . . . (London, 1604), in *Somers Tracts*, II, 96.
5. Ibid., p. 77.
6. Sir Ralph Winwood, *Memorials of the Affairs of State in the Reigns of Queen Elizabeth and King James I* (London, 1725), II, 76.
7. *Calendar of State Papers, Venetian, 1607–1610*, p. 6.
8. Ibid., *1610–1613*, p. 335.   9. Gardiner, I, 212.
10. *Tom Tell-Troath, or a free Discourse touching the Manners of the Time. Directed to His Majesty by waye of humble advertisement* (n.p., n.d.), in *Somers Tracts*, II, 472.
11. Charles Howard Carter, *The Secret Diplomacy of the Habsburgs, 1598–1625* (New York, 1964), p. 133.
12. Garrett Mattingly, *Renaissance Diplomacy* (Boston, 1955), pp. 262–266.
13. *Observations concerning the present affairs of Holland and the United Provinces by an English Gentleman* (St. Omer, 1621?).
14. *Commons Debates, 1621*, eds. W. Notestein, F. H. Relf, and H. Simpson (New Haven, 1935), III, 465–468.
15. Ibid., p. 469.   17. Ibid., I, 637.
16. Ibid,. IV, 441.   18. Davies, pp. 27–28.
19. *Niuew Nederlandsch Biografisch Woordenboek* (Leiden, 1918), IV, 1242.

William Steven, *The History of the Scottish Church, Rotterdam* (Edinburgh, 1832), p. 338.

20. *Calendar of State Papers, Domestic, 1619–1623*, p. 462.
21. Ibid., p. 468.
22. *Dictionary of National Biography*, XVIII, 1006.
23. [Thomas Scott], *Vox Populi, or Newes from Spayne, translated according to the Spanish coppie* . . . (n.p., 1620), in *Somers Tracts*, II, 510–511.
24. Ibid., pp. 515–517.
25. Ibid., p. 513.   26. Ibid., p. 520.
27. [Thomas Scott], *The Second Part of Vox Populi, or Gondomar appearing in the likeness of Matchiauell* . . . , 2nd ed. (n.p., 1624), pp. 13–14.
28. Ibid., p. 12.   29. Ibid., p. 7.
30. [Thomas Scott], *Sir Walter Raleigh's Ghost: or England's Forewarner* . . . (Utrecht, 1626), in *Somers Tracts*, II, 532.
31. Ibid., pp. 539–546.   32. Ibid., p. 534.
33. [Thomas Scott], *Vox Coeli, or News from Heaven* . . . (n.p., 1624), in *Somers Tracts*, II, 580.
34. Ibid., pp. 564–581.
35. Ibid., p. 567.   38. Ibid., p. 585.
36. Ibid., p. 569.   39. Ibid., p. 570.
37. Ibid., pp. 563–564.   40. Ibid., pp. 588–590.
41. [Thomas Scott], *Robert Earl of Essex his Ghost, sent from Elizian* . . . (n.p., 1642), in *Somers Tracts*, II, 604.
42. Ibid., pp. 602–603.
43. [Thomas Scott], *A Postscript, or a Second Part of Robert Earle of Essex his Ghost* (n.p., 1642), in *Somers Tracts*, II, 604.
44. [Thomas Scott], *A Tongue-Combat, Lately Happening between tvvo English Souldiers in the Tilt-boat of Gravesend* (London, 1623), p. 80.
45. *An Experimental Discoverie of Spanish Practises, or, The Counsell of a well-wishing Souldier, for the good of his Prince and State* (n.p., 1623), pp. 30–31.
46. Ibid., p. 32.   47. Ibid., p. 31. Ellipses in original.
48. Scott, *Sir Walter Raleigh's Ghost*, p. 545; Scott, *The Second Part of Vox Populi*, p. 14.
49. Gardiner, III, 393.
50. Scott, *The Second Part of Vox Populi*, p. 26. Scott's *Vox Coeli* was so favorable to Buckingham that Sir Walter Scott thought it was written under the latter's personal direction. *Somers Tracts*, II, 555.
51. Richard Peeke (or Pike), *Three to One. Being an English-Spanish Combat performed by a Western Gentleman of Tavistock* . . . (London, 1626), in C. H. Firth, ed., *Stuart Tracts, 1603–1693* (Westminster, 1903), p. 290.
52. *A Panegyric Poem, or Tavistock's Encomium*, which the present author has been unable to locate.
53. *Dick of Devonshire* (London, 1626?) in Malone Society Reprints (Oxford, 1955), act 1, sc. 2.
54. Peeke, pp. 282–283.
55. *A True Relation of a Brave English Stratagem practised lately upon a sea town in Galicia* . . . (n.p., 1626), in *Stuart Tracts*, pp. 306–307.

56. Davies, p. 63.
57. *Miles Gloriosus, the Spanish Braggadocio: Or, the humour of the Spaniard*, trans. I. W. (London, 1630), p. 1.
58. *The Wicked Plots and Perfidious Practices of the Spaniards against the Seventeen Provinces of the Netherlands, before they took up Arms . . .* (n.p., 1642), in *Harleian Miscellany*, V, 172–182.
59. Thomas Allured, *The Copie of a Letter Written to the Duke of Buckingham Concerning the match with Spaine* (London, 1642), pp. 3–7.
60. G. B. C. *Plots, Conspiracies and Attempts of Domestick and Forraigne Enemies of the Romish Religion* (London, 1642).
61. H. C. *Englands Present Distractions Paralleled with those of Spaine and other forraine Countries* (London, 1642), pp. 4–5.
62. *Dictionary of National Biography*, XX, 1073.
63. Sir Anthony Weldon, *The Court and Character of King James* (London, 1651) in *Secret History of the Court of James I* (Edinburgh, 1811), I, 354.
64. Ibid., pp. 355–356.
65. Ibid., pp. 356–358.   66. Ibid., p. 358.
67. Arthur Wilson, *The History of Great Britain, being the Life and Reign of King James the First* (London, 1653), p. 91.
68. Ibid., p. 92.   69. Ibid., p. 75.

CHAPTER IX. THE FRUITS OF HATRED

1. S. R. Gardiner, *History of the Commonwealth and Protectorate, 1649–1656* (London, 1903), III, 164.
2. Ibid., p. 163.
3. *The Clarke Papers*, ed. C. H. Firth (London, 1899), III, 203.
4. Ibid., p. 206.   5. Ibid., p. 207.
6. Ibid., p. 208. For a general discussion of Cromwell's motives in the "Western Design" see Frank Strong, "The Causes of Cromwell's West Indian Expedition," *American Historical Review*, II (1899), 228–245.
7. Thomas Carlyle, *The Letters and Speeches of Oliver Cromwell* (London, 1904), II, 511.
8. Ibid., p. 514.
9. *A Declaration of His Hignes By the Advice of His Council, Setting forth On the Behalf of this Commonwealth, the Justice of their Cause against Spain* (London, 1655), pp. 12–128.
10. Ibid., p. 123.
11. Ibid., p. 125.   14. Ibid., p. 140.
12. Ibid., p. 118.   15. Ibid., p. 118.
13. Ibid., pp. 119–120.   16. Ibid., p. 142.
17. In *The Prose Works of John Milton*, ed. R. W. Griswold (Philadelphia, 1856), II, 465–468.
18. *A Dialogue, Containing a Compendious Discourse concerning the Present Designe in the West Indies* (London, 1655), p. 8.
19. Ibid., p. 10.
20. *A Brief and perfect Journal of the late Proceedings and Successe of the English Army in the West Indies*, by I. S. (London, 1655), p. 4.

21. *A Collection of the State Papers of John Thurloe, Esq.*, ed. Thomas Birch (London, 1742), III, 69, contains the complete text.
22. Gardiner, *History of the Commonwealth and Protectorate*, IV, 123.
23. *A Lamentable Narration of the sad Disaster of a great part of the Spanish Plate Fleet* ... (London, 1658). Single sheet.
24. *Publick Intelligencer* (December 31–January 7, 1655), pp. 226–231.
25. Ibid. (April 7–14, 1656), p. 479.
26. *Mercurius Politicus* (April 24–May 1, 1656), pp. 6938–6939.
27. *The King of Spains Cabinet Council Divulged; or a Discovery of the Prevarications of the Spaniards*, by J. H. (London, 1658), pp. 50–52.
28. *Englands Present Distractions Paralleled with those of Spaine and other forraine Countries* (London, 1642).
29. *The King of Spains Cabinet Council Divulged*, p. 64.
30. Ibid., p. 66.
31. Ibid., p. 68.   32. Ibid., p. 67.
33. J. H. Elliott, *The Revolt of the Catalans* (Cambridge, 1963), pp. 370–373.
34. Ibid., p. 395.   35. Ibid., p. 458.
36. *The King of Spains Cabinet Council Divulged*, pp. 30–31.
37. Ibid., p. 28.   38. Ibid., p. 29.
39. *Dictionary of National Biography* V, 554.
40. Ibid., p. 555.
41. Sir William D'Avenant, *The Cruelty of the Spaniards in Peru* (London, 1658), p. 8.
42. Ibid., p. 19.   44. Ibid., pp. 23–24.
43. Ibid., pp. 21–22.   45. Ibid., p. 27.
46. Sir William D' Avenant, *The History of Sir Francis Drake* (London, 1659), p. 29.
47. Sir Ferdinando Gorges, *America Painted to the Life* ... (London, 1659), p. A2.
48. *America: or An exact Description of the West-Indies*, by N. N. (London, 1655), pp. 216–217.
49. Ibid., p. 280.   50. Ibid., p. 287.

CHAPTER X. CONCLUSION

1. *The Character of Spain: Or, An Epitome of Their Virtues and Vices* (London, 1660), p. 1.
2. Ibid., p. 76.   5. Ibid., p. 10.
3. Ibid., p. 73.   6. Ibid., pp. 36–37.
4. Ibid., p. 3.   7. Ibid., p. 71.

SELECTED BIBLIOGRAPHY

Acosta, José de. *The Natural and Moral History of the Indies.* Trans. Edward Grimston, ed. Clements R. Markham. London: Hakluyt Society, 1880.

Acts of the Privy Council of England, new series. Ed. J. R. Dasent. London: Her Majesty's Stationary Office, 1890.

Advertisements of a loyal Subject to his gracious Sovereign, drawn from the Observations of the People's Speeches. Never printed independently. In: *Somers Tracts.* Ed. Walter Scott. 2nd ed. London: T. Cadell et al., 1809. II, 144.

Allured, Thomas. *The Copie of a Letter Written to the Duke of Buckingham Concerning the match with Spaine.* London: George Tomlinson, 1642.

America: or An exact Description of the West-Indies. By N. N. London: Ric. Hodgkensonne for Edward Dod, 1655.

Arnoldsson, Sverker. *La Conquista Española de América, según la juicio de la posteridad: Vestigios de la Leyenda Negra.* Madrid: Insula, 1960.

―――. *La Leyenda Negra: Estudios sobre sus orígenes.* Göteborg: Göteborgs *Universitets Arsskrift.* LXVI, 1960.

Baker, Sir Richard. *A Chronicle of the Kings of England.* London: George Sawbridge, 1679.

Bataillon, Marcel. *Erasmo y España.* Trans. Antonio Alatorre. 2 vols. Mexico: Fondo de Cultura Económica, 1950.

Bennett, H. S. *English Books and Readers, 1475–1557.* Cambridge: Cambridge University Press, 1952.

Billingsly, Nicholas. *Brachy-Martyrologia: or, a Breviary of all the Greatest Persecutions Which have befallen the Saints and People of God.* London: J. C. for Austin Rice, 1657.

Black, J. B. *The Reign of Elizabeth.* Oxford: Clarendon Press, 1959.

Borah, Woodrow W., and Sherburne F. Cook. *The Aboriginal Population of Central Mexico on the Eve of the Spanish Conquest.* Berkeley: University of California Press, 1963.

Bowman, J. N. *The Protestant Interest in Cromwell's Foreign Relations.* Heidelberg: Carl Winter, 1900.

Bradford, John. *The Copye of a Letter, sent by John Bradforth to the right honorable lordes the Erles of Arundel, Darbie, Shrewsburye, and Pembroke, declaring the nature of the Spaniardes, and discovering the most detestable treasons which thei have pretended moste falselye agaynste our moste noble kingdome of Englande.* N.p., n.d. [1556].

A Brief and perfect Journal of the late Proceedings and Successe of the English Army in the West Indies. By I. S. London: 1655.

A Briefe Chronicle, and perfect rehearsal of all the memorable actions happened not onlie in the low Countries, but also in Germanie, Italy, France, Spaine, England, Turkie and other Countries since the yeare of our Lord 1500 to the present yeare, 1598. London: John Wolfe, 1598.

A Briefe Description of the Battailes, Victories and Triumphes, atchieved by the D. of Parma, and the Spanish Army. London: Edward White, 1591.

A briefe relation, of what is happened since the last of August 1598 by comming of the Spanish campe into the Dukedome of Cleve and the bordering free Countries, which with most odious and barbarous crueltie they take as enemies for the service of God and the King of Spaine (as they say). Trans. from the Dutch. London: John Wolfe, 1599.

Brooks, Mary Elizabeth. *A King for Portugal.* Madison, Wis.: University of Wisconsin Press, 1964.

Calendar of State Papers. Domestic.

Calendar of State Papers. Spanish.

Calendar of State Papers. Venetian.

Camden, William. *The History of the Most Renowned and Victorious Princess Elizabeth, Late Queen of England.* 4th ed. London: M. Flesher for J. Tonson, 1688.

Cárbia, Rómulo D. *Historia de la Leyenda Negra Hispano-Americana.* Buenos Aires: Ediciones Orientación Española, 1943.

Carlyle, Thomas. *The Letters and Speeches of Oliver Cromwell.* Ed. S. C. Lomas. London: Methuen, 1904.

Carter, Charles Howard. *The Secret Diplomacy of the Habsburgs, 1598–1625.* New York: Columbia University Press, 1964.

Cawley, R. R. *Unpathed Waters: Studies in the Influence of the Voyagers on Elizabethan Literature.* New York: Octagon Books, 1967.

———. *The Voyagers and Elizabethan Drama.* Boston: D. C. Heath, 1938.

[Cecil, William (Lord Burghley).] *The Copy of a Letter Sent Out of England to Don Bernardin Mendoza, Ambassador in France for the*

King of Spain, declaring the State of England. London: J. Vautrollier for Richard Field, 1588. In *Harleian Miscellany*. Ed. T. Park. London: Robert Dutton, 1808–1813. II, 60–85.

——. *A declaration of the favorable dealing of her Majestie's commissioners, appointed for the examination of certayne traytors, and of tortures unjustly reported to be done upon them for matter of religion.* 1583. In *Somers Tracts*, I, 209–212.

Certain Advertisements out of Ireland, concerning the losses and distresses happened to the Spanish Navy upon the West Coasts of Ireland. London: J. Vautrollier for Richard Field, 1588. In *Harleian Miscellany*, II, 47–59.

Chamberlain, R. S. *Castilian Backgrounds of the Repartimiento-Encomienda*, Carnegie Institution Publications, no. 509. 1939. Pp. 15–66.

The Character of Spain: Or, An Epitome of Their Virtues and Vices. London: Nath. Brooke, 1660.

Churchyard, Thomas. *A Lamentable and pitiful Description of the wofull warres in Flaunders, since the foure last yeares of the Emperour Charles the fifth, his raigne.* London: Ralph Newberrie, 1578.

Clark, Samuel. *England's Remembrancer.* London: J. G. for John Rothwell, 1657. In *Smeeton's Historical and Biographical Tracts.* Vol. I. Westminster, 1819.

The Clarke Papers. Ed. C. H. Firth. Camden Society, Vol. LXI. London: Longmans, Green, 1899.

Codrington, Robert. *The Life and Death of the Illustrious Robert, Earl of Essex.* London: F. Leach for L. Chapman, 1646. In *Harleian Miscellany*, VI, 3–35.

Colección de documentos inéditos de Indias. Madrid, 1864–1884.

Commons Debates, 1621. Ed. W. Notestein, F. H. Relf, and H. Simpson. New Haven: Yale University Press, 1935.

The Conquest of the Grand Canaries, made this last Summer . . . London: P. S. for William Apsley, 1599.

The Coppie of the Anti-Spaniard made at Paris by a French man, a Catholique, Wherein is directly proved how the Spanish king is the onely cause of all the troubles in France. Trans. out of the French into English. London: John Wolfe, 1590.

The Coppie of a Letter sent into England by a Gentleman from the towne of Saint Denis in France. Wherein is truely set forth the good success of the King Maiesties forces against the Leaugers and the Prince of Parmas power. London: Thomas Scarlet for Thomas Nelson, 1590.

Corbett, Julian S. *Drake and the Tudor Navy*. London: Longmans, Green, 1899.

Cotton, Sir Robert. *A Choice Narrative of Count Gondomar's Transactions during his Embassy in England*. London: John Garfield, 1659. (A reissue of *Vox Populi*.)

D'Antas, Miguel. *Les faux Don Sebastien*. Paris: Chez Auguste Durand, Libraire, 1866.

D'Avenant, Sir William. *The Cruelty of the Spaniards in Peru. A masque in 6 parts*. London: Henry Herringman, 1658.

———. *The History of Sir Francis Drake*. London: Henry Herringman, 1659.

Davies, Godfrey. *The Early Stuarts, 1603-1660*. Oxford: Clarendon Press, 1959.

Dean, Leonard F. "Tudor Theories of History Writing," *University of Michigan Contributions in Modern Philology*, no. 1 (April, 1947), pp. 1–24.

A Declaration of the Causes moving Her Majesty to send an army to the Seas. London: Christopher Barker, 1596.

A Declaration of the Causes Moving the Queen of England to give aide to the Defence of the People afflicted and oppressed in the Lowe Countries, 1585, together with an Addition to the Declaration, touching the Slanders published of her Majestie. Given at Richmoun the first of October, 1585. In *Somers Tracts*, I, 410–420.

A Declaration of the Causes which mooved the chiefe Commanders of the Navie of her most excellent Maiestie the Queen of England, in their voyage and expedition to Portingal, to take and arrest in the mouth of the River of Lisbone, certaine Shippes of corne and other provisions of warre bound for the said Citie. London: Christopher Barker, 1589.

A Declaration of His Highnes By the Advice of His Council, Setting forth On the Behalf of this Commonwealth, the Justice of their Cause against Spain. London: Henry Hills and John Field, 1655.

A Declaration to the People. London: G. E. Horton, 1659.

A Declaration & Publication of the Prince of Orange. Contayning the cause of his necessary defense against the Duke of Alva (20 July, 1568). Trans. out of the French. London: J. Day, 1568?

Deloney, Thomas. *An Excellant Song on the Winning of Cales by the*

English. In C. H. Firth, *Naval Songs and Ballads*, Navy Record Society. 1908. XXXIII, 21–23.

———. *A Joyfull new Ballad declaring the happy obtaining of the great Galleazzo, wherein Don Pedro Valdez was the Chief*. London: John Wolfe for Edward White, 1588. In Edward Arber, *An English Garner, Tudor Tracts, 1532–1588*. Westminister: Archibald Constable, 1903.

———. *A new Ballet of the strange and most cruel whips, which the Spaniards had prepared to whip and torment English men and women: which were found and taken at the overthrow of certain Spanish ships, in July last past, 1588*. London: Thomas Orwin and Thomas Gubbin, 1588. In *An English Garner, Tudor Tracts, 1532–1588*, pp. 498–502.

A Dialogue, Containing a Compendious Discourse concerning the Present Designe in the West Indies. London: R. Lowndes, 1655.

Díaz del Castillo, Bernal. *Historia verdadera de la Conquista de la Nueva España*. 2 vols. Madrid: Espasa-Calpe, 1933.

Dick of Devonshire. London: 1626; Oxford: Malone Society Reprints, 1955.

Dictionary of National Biography. Ed. Sir Leslie Stephen and Sir Sidney Lee. London: Oxford University Press.

Dierickx, M., S.J. "La politique religieuse de Philippe II dans les anciens Pays-bas," *Hispania*, XVI (1956), 131–143.

A discourse of the present state of the Wars in the lowe Countries. Wherein is contayned the pitiful spoyle of Askot: And the Articles of Peace to be concluded betweene the States and Don John de Austria. London: W. B., 1578.

A Discourse of the usage of the English Fugitives by the Spaniard. London: Thomas Scarlet for John Drawater, 1595.

Eibling, Harold H., King, Fred M., and Harlow, James. *Our United States: A Bulwark of Freedom*. River Forest, Ill.: Laidlaw Brothers, 1962.

Elliott, J. H. *The Revolt of the Catalans*. Cambridge: Cambridge University Press, 1963.

Englands Present Distractions Paralleled with those of Spaine and other forraine Countries. By H. C.; B. L. C. London: Francis Wright, 1642.

The Estate of the English Fugitives under the king of Spaine and his ministers. London: Thomas Scarlet for John Drawater, 1595.

An Experimental Discoverie of Spanish Practises, or, The Counsell of a well-wishing Souldier for the good of his Prince and State. N.p., 1623.

A Fig for the Spaniard. By G. B. London: John Wolfe, 1591.

Firth, C. H. *The Last Years of the Protectorate, 1656–1658.* 2 vols. London: Longmans, Green, 1909.

Fletcher, Francis. *The World Encompassed by Sir Francis Drake.* London: Nicholas Brown, 1628. In *Hakluyt Society*, ser. 1, no. 16, 1854.

Foxe, John. *Acts and Monuments.* Ed. Stephen Reed Cattley. 8 vols. London: R. B. Seeley and W. Burnside, 1839.

Gage, Thomas. *The English-American his Travail by Sea and Land: or, A New Survey of the West Indies.* London: R. Cotes for Humphrey Blunden and Thomas Williams, 1648.

Gardiner, S. R. *History of the Commonwealth and Protectorate, 1649–1656.* 4 vols. London: Longmans, Green, 1903.

———. *History of England from the Accession of James I to the Outbreak of the Civil War.* 10 vols. London: Longmans, Green, 1896.

Gascoigne, George. *The Spoil of Antwerp. Faithfully reported by a true Englishman who was present at the same.* London: Richard Jones, 1576. In *An English Garner, Tudor Tracts, 1532–1588,* pp. 419–449.

[Gentilys, Robert.] *The French-man and the Spaniard, or The two Great Lights of the World.* London: Humphrey Moseley, 1642.

Geyl, Pieter. *The Revolt of the Netherlands, 1555-1609.* New York: Barnes and Noble, 1958.

Gómara, Francisco López de. *The Pleasant Historie of the Conquest of the VVest India, now called new Spayne, atchiued by the vvorthy Prince Hernando Cortes Marquess of the valley of Huaxacas, most delectable to read.* Translated out of the Spanishe tongue by T. N. London: Henry Bynneman, 1578.

Gonsalvius Montanus, Reginald. *A Discovery and playne Declaration of sundry subtill practises of the Holy Inquisition of Spain.* London: Ihon Day, 1568.

Gorges, Sir Ferdinando. *America Painted to the Life. The History of the Spaniards Proceedings in America.* London: T. J. for Nath. Brook, 1659.

Greene, Robert. *The Spanish Masquerado.* London: Roger Ward, 1589.

Groff, Henry F., and Krout, John A. *The Adventure of the American People.* New York: Rand McNally, 1961.

Grossman, Rudolph. *Spanien und das elisabethanische Drama.* Hamburg: L. Friedrichsen, 1920.

Guerts, P. A. M. *De Nederlandse Opstand in de Pamfletten, 1566–1584.* Nijmegen-Utrecht: Dekker and van de Vegt, N.V., 1956.

Guicciardini, Francesco. *The Historie of Guicciardin, conteining the warres of Italy.* Trans. Geoffrey Fenton. London: Richard Field, 1599.

Hakluyt, Richard (the Elder). *Inducements to the Liking of the Voyage intended towards Virginia in 40. and 42. degrees of latitude.* London: 1585. In *The Writings and Correspondence of the Two Richard Hakluyts.* Ed. E. G. R. Taylor. London: Hakluyt Society, ser. 2, no. 77, 1935, pp. 327–338.

Hakluyt, Richard. *A Discourse concerning Western Planting.* Ed. Charles Deane. Cambridge: John Wilson and Son, 1877.

———. *Divers Voyages Touching the Discouerie of America and the Ilands Adiacent.* London: Thomas Woodcocke, 1582.

———. *The Principle Voyages, Traffiques & Discoveries of the English Nation.* 12 vols. Glasgow: James MacLehose and Sons, 1904.

Haller, William. *The Elect Nation: The Meaning and Relevance of Foxe's Book of Martyr's.* New York: Harper and Row, 1963.

Hanke, Lewis. *Aristotle and the American Indians.* Chicago: Henry Regnery, 1959.

———. *Bartolomé de Las Casas: Bookman, Scholar, and Propagandist.* Philadelphia: University of Pennsylvania Press, 1952.

———. *Bartolomé de Las Casas: Historian.* Gainesville, Fla.: University of Florida Press, 1952.

———. *Bartolomé de Las Casas: An Interpretation of His Life and Writings.* The Hague: Martinus Nijhoff, 1951.

———. *The Spanish Struggle for Justice in the Conquest of America.* Philadelphia: University of Pennsylvania Press, 1949.

Haring, C. H. *The Spanish Empire in America.* New York: Oxford University Press, 1947.

Haslop, Henry. *Newes out of the Coast of Spaine.* London: W. How for Henry Haslop, 1587.

Hawkins, Sir John. *A true declaration of the troublesome voyadge of M. J. Hawkins to the parties of Guynea and the west-Indies.* London: T. Purfoote for L. Harrison, 1569. reprinted in Hakluyt, *Principle Voyages,* X, 64–74.

Helps, Arthur. *The Life of Las Casas, "The Apostle of the Indies."* London: Bell and Daldy, 1868.

An Historical Discourse, or rather a Tragicall Historie of the citie of Antwerpe. London: John Windet, 1586.

Selected Bibliography

Historical Manuscripts Commission. *Calendar of the Manuscripts of the Most Honourable, the Marquis of Salisbury, K. G. preserved at Hatfield House, Hertfordshire.* London, 1894.

Holinshed, Raphael. *Chronicles of England, Scotland, and Ireland.* 6 vols. London: J. Johnson, F. C. and J. Rivington, T. Payne, Wilkie and Robinson, Longman, Hurst, Rees and Orme, Cadell and Davies, and J. Mawman, 1808.

Hortop, Job. *The travailes of an Englishman.* London: T. Scarlet for W. Wright, 1591. Reprinted in Hakluyt, *Principle Voyages,* IX, 452–489.

Howes, Edmund. *Annales, or a Generall Chronicle of England. Begun by John Stow: Continued and Augmented . . . unto the end of this present yeere, 1631.* London: Richard Meighan, 1631.

Jenkins, Gladys. "Ways and Means in Elizabethan Propaganda," *History,* XXVI (1941), 105–114.

Juderías, Julián. *La Leyenda Negra.* 4th ed. Barcelona: Casa Editorial Araluce, 1917.

A Justification or cleering of the Prince of Orendge agaynst the false sclaunders, wherwith his ilwillers goe about to charge him wrongfully. London: John Day, 1573.

Kamen, Henry. *The Spanish Inquisition.* London: Weidenfeld and Nicolson, 1965.

The King of Spains Cabinet Council Divulged; or a Discovery of the Prevarications of the Spaniards. By J. H. for J. S. to be sold by Simon Miller. London, 1658.

Klein, A. J. *Intolerance in the Reign of Elizabeth, Queen of England.* Boston and New York: Houghton Mifflin, 1917.

Knuttel, W. P. C. *Catalogus van de Pamfletten-Versameling berustende de Koninklijke Bibliothek.* 8 vols. The Hague: Gedrikt ter Algemeine Landsdrukkerij, 1889.

Kyd, Thomas. *The Spanish Tragedie: or Hieronimo is mad againe.* London: W. White for I. White and I. Langley, 1615. In *The Works of Thomas Kyd.* Ed. Frederick S. Boas. Oxford: Clarendon Press, 1955.

A Lamentable Narration of the sad Disaster of a great part of the Spanish Plate Fleet that perished near St. Lucas. London: T. F. for N. B., 1658.

A Larum for London or the Siedge of Antwerpe, With the ventrous actes and valorous deeds of the lame soldier. As it hath been playde by the right Homorable the Lord Chamberlaine his Servants. London: William Ferbrand, 1602. Ed. W. W. Greg. Malone Society Reprints, 1913.

Las Casas, Bartolomé de. *The Spanish Colonie, or Briefe Chronicle of the Acts and Gestes of the Spaniards in the West Indies, called the New World for the space of xl. yeares.* Trans. M. M. S. London: William Brome, 1583.

Laudonnière, René de. *A notable historie containing foure voyages made by certayne French captaynes into Florida.* Trans. Richard Hakluyt. London: T. Dawson, 1587.

Lea, Henry Charles. *A History of the Inquisition of Spain.* 4 vols. New York: Macmillan, 1922.

———. *The Inquisition in the Spanish Dependencies.* New York: Macmillan, 1907.

LeChalleaux, Nicholas. *A True and perfect description of the last voyage or Navigation, attempted by Capitaine John Rybaut.* London: Henry Denham for Thomas Hacket, 1565.

A Letter Written upon Occasion in the Low-countries. London: Nathanial Butter, 1641.

Lewkenor, Sir Lewis. *A Discourse of the Usage of the English Fugitives by the Spaniard.* London: Thomas Scarlet for John Drawater, 1595.

Lindabury, Richard V. *A Study of Patriotism in the Elizabethan Drama.* Princeton: Princeton University Press, 1931.

Linschoten, Jan Huyghen van. *J. H. van Linschoten his discours of voyages into ye Easte and West Indies.* Trans. W. Phillip. London: J. Wolfe, 1598.

Livermore, H. V. *A History of Portugal.* Cambridge: Cambridge University Press, 1947.

Loomie, Albert J., S. J. *The Spanish Elizabethans.* New York: Fordham University Press, 1963.

———. *Toleration and Diplomacy: The Religious Issue in Anglo-Spanish Relations, 1603–1605.* Transactions of the American Philosophical Society. Vol. LIII, part 6. Philadelphia, 1963.

Lyly, John. *Midas.* London: Thomas Scarlet for I. B., 1592. In *The Complete Works of John Lyly.* Ed. R. Warwick Bond. Oxford: Clarendon Press, 1902. III, 105–162.

Lyman, Edward, ed. *Richard Hakluyt and His Successors.* London: Hakluyt Society, ser. 2, no. 93, 1946.

Lynch, John. *Spain under the Habsburgs.* Oxford: Basil Blackwell, 1964.

Machiavelli, Niccolò. *The arte of Warre.* Trans. Peter Whitehorne. London: Ihon Kingston for Nicholas Englande, 1562.

————. *I Discorsi de Nicolo Machiavelli, sopra la prima deca de Tito Livio.* London: J. Wolfe, 1584.

————. *The Florentine historie.* Trans. T. B. London: T. C. for VV. P., 1595.

————. *Il Principe de Nicolo Machiavelli . . . Con Alcune altre operette.* London: J. Wolfe, 1584.

Marañón, Gregorio. *Antonio Pérez.* Madrid: Espasa-Calpe, S. A., 1954.

Marten, Anthony. *An Exhortation to stir up the minds of All Her Majesty's Faithful Subjects to defend their Country, in this dangerous Time, from the Invasion of Enemies.* London: John Windet, 1588. In *Harleian Miscellany*, II, 85–107.

Mattingly, Garrett. *The Armada.* Boston: Houghton Mifflin, 1959.

————. *Renaissance Diplomacy.* Boston: Houghton Mifflin, 1955.

Maynarde, Thomas. *Sir Francis Drake, His Voyage, 1595.* Ed. W. D. Cooley. London: Hakluyt Society, ser. 1 no. 4, 1849.

Merriman, Roger Bigelow. *The Rise of the Spanish Empire.* 4 vols. New York: Macmillan, 1934.

Mercurius Politicus.

Meteren, Emanuel van. *Historia Belgica Nostri Potissimum Temporis.* N.p., n.d.

————. *A True Discourse Historicall of the succeeding governours in the Netherlands and the ciuill warres there begun in the yeere 1565.* Trans. Thomas Churchyard and Ric. Ro. [Richard Robinson]. London: Matthew Lownes, 1602.

Meyer, A. O. *England and the Catholic Church under Elizabeth.* Trans. J. R. McKee. London: Kegan Paul, Trench, Trubner, 1916.

Middleton, Thomas. *A Game at Chesse.* Ed. R. C. Bald. Cambridge: Cambridge University Press, 1929.

Miles Gloriosus, the Spanish Braggadocio: Or, the humour of the Spaniard. Trans. I. W. printed in both French and English. London: T. H. for I. E., 1630.

[Milton, John.] *The Prose Works of John Milton.* Ed. Rufus Wilmot Griswold. 2 vols. Philadelphia: J. W. Moore, 1856.

Motley, John Lothrop. *The Rise of the Dutch Republic.* 3 vols. New York: Harper and Brothers, 1855.

Nashe, Thomas. *Pierce Pennilesse His Supplication to the Divell.* London: John Lane The Bodley Head, 1924.

Newes from Antwerp, the. 10. day of August. 1580. London: John Charlewood, 1580.

Newes from France where Monsieur de Signiers in the Kings behalfe most brauely discomfited the army of the King of Spain and the Pope. London: Thomas Scarlet for William Wright, 1591.

Newes out of France on the First of this moneth of March. London: John Wolfe, 1592.

Newes of the Netherlands, Relating to the whole state of those Countries at this Present. London: Felix Kingston for Edward Marchant, 1615.

Orders Set Down by the Duke of Medina, Lord General of the King's Fleet, to be observed in the voyage towards England by T. P. London: Thomas Orwin for Thomas Gilbert, 1588. In *Harleian Miscellany*, II, 42–47.

Overbury, Sir Thomas. *Sir Thomas Overbury, His Observations in his Travels, Upon the State of the Seventeen Provinces, as they stood anno domini, 1609.* London: J. Parker, 1626. In *Stuart Tracts, 1603–1693.* Ed. C. H. Firth. Westminster: Archibald Constable, 1903. Pp. 211–232.

A Packe of Spanish Lyes sent Abroad in the World. London: By the deputies of Christopher Barker, Printer to the Queenes most excellent Maiestie, 1588. In *Harleian Miscellany*, II, 177–129.

A Pageant of Spanish Humours. Translated out of Dutche by H. W. London: John Wolfe, 1599.

Parks, George Bruner. *Richard Hakluyt and the English Voyages.* New York: American Geographical Society, 1928.

Peeke (or Pike), Richard. *Three to one. Being an English-Spanish Combat performed by a Western Gentleman of Tavistock in Devonshire with an English quarterstaff, against three Spaniards (at once) with rapiers and poniards . . . .* London: J. T. [John Trundle], 1626. In *Stuart Tracts, 1603–1693.* Ed. C. H. Firth. Westminister: Archibald Constable, 1903, pp. 275–347.

Perez, Antonio. *Pedaços de Historia, o Relaciones, assy llamadas por sus Auctores los Peregrinos.* No place, publisher, or date.

[———?] *The Spanish Pilgrime: or an Admirable Discovery of a Romish Catholicke.* London: B. A[lsop]., sold by T. Archer, 1625.

———. *A Treatise Paraenetical, That is to say: An Exhortation. Wherein is showed by good and evident reasons, infallible arguments, most true and certaine histories, and notable examples; the right way and true means to resist the violence of the Castilian king: to break the course of his desseignes: to beat down his pride, and to ruinate his puissance.* London: William Ponsonby, 1598.

Peter Martyr d'Anghiera. *The Decades of the Newe Worlde, or West India conteyning the navigations and conquestes of the Spaniardes.* Trans. Richard Eden. London: William Powell, 1555. In *The First Three English Books on America.* Ed. Edward Arber. Westminster: Archibald Constable, 1895.

Pirenne, Henri. *Histoire de Belgique.* 7 vols. Brussels: Maurice Lambertin, 1927.

Plots, Conspiracies and Attempts of Domestick and Forraigne Enemies of the Romish Religion. By G. B. C. London: Ralph Rounthwaite, 1642.

Pollen, J. H. *The English Catholics in the Reign of Queen Elizabeth, 1558–1580.* London: Longmans, Green, 1920.

The Present State of Spain. Translated out of the French. London: P. S. for Richard Serger, 1594.

Proclamation of the Lords of the Generall States of the united Provinces, whereby the Spaniards and all their goods are declared to be lawfull prize. Translated from the Dutch. London: John Wolfe, 1599.

Publick Intelligencer.

Purchas, Samuel. *Hakluytus Posthumus, or Purchas His Pilgrimes.* 20 vols. Glasgow: James MacLehose and Sons, 1906.

Quevedo y Villegas, Francisco Gómez de. *Obras completas.* Ed. Don Aureliano Fernandez-Guerra y Orbe. Sevilla: Sociedad de Bibliófilas Andaluces, 1897.

Randall, Dale B. J. *The Golden Tapestry: A Critical Survey of Non-chivalric Spanish Fiction in English Translation.* Durham, N.C.: Duke University Press, 1963.

Raleigh, Sir Walter. *The discouerie of the large rich, and bewtiful empire of Guiana. Performed in the year 1595, by Sir Walter Raleigh.* London: R. Robinson, 1596. Reprinted in Hakluyt, *Principle Voyages,* Vol. X.

———. *The History of the World.* London, 1687.

———. *Judicious and Select Essays and Observations.* London: T. W. for Humphrey Mosele, 1650.

———. *A report of the truth of the fight about the iles of Açores.* London: William Ponsonbie, 1591.

Read, Conyers. "William Cecil and Elizabethan Public Relations." *Elizabethan Government and Society: Essays presented to Sir John Neale.* Ed. S. T. Bindoff, J. Hurstfield, and C. H. Williams. London: Athlone Press, 1961.

A Relation of a Voyage to Guiana, Performed by Robert Harcourt.

London: John Beale for W. Welby, 1613. In *Harleian Miscellany*, III, 169–212.

Rowse, A. L. *The Expansion of Elizabethan England*. New York: St. Martin's Press, 1955.

Sanderson, Sir William, *A Compleat History of the Lives and Reigns of Mary Queen of Scotland and of her Son and Successor, James*. London: Humphrey Mosely, Richard Tomlins, and George Sawbridge, 1642.

Schäfer, Ernest. *Beiträge zur Geschichte des spanischen Protestantismus und der Inquisition*. Gütersloh: Druck und Verlag von C. Bertelsmann, 1902.

Schwartz, Melvin, and O'Connor, John. *Exploring American History*. New York: Globe, 1963.

[Scott, Thomas.] *Certaine Reasons and Arguments of Policie, Why the King of England should hereafter give over all further Treatie, and enter into warre with the Spaniard*. N.p., 1624.

[———.] *An Experimental Discoverie of Spanish Practises, or, The Counsell of a well-wishing Souldier, for the good of his Prince and State*. N.p., 1623.

[———.] *Newes from Pernassus. Printed at Helicon*, 1622.

[———.] *A Postscript, or a Second Part of Robert Earle of Essex his Ghost. To the Nobility, Gentry, and Communality of England. Printed in Paradise*, 1642. In *Somers Tracts*, II, 604–608.

[———.] *Robert Earl of Essex his Ghost, sent from Elizian: To the Nobility, Gentry and Communalitye of England. Printed in Paradise*, 1624. In *Somers Tracts*, II, 596–603.

[———.] *The Second Part of Vox Populi, or Gondomar appearing in the likeness of Matchiauell in a Spanish Parliament, wherein are discovered his treacherous and subtile Practices To the ruine as well of England, as the Netherlands. Faithfully translated out of the Spanish Coppie by a well-willer to England and Holland*. 2nd ed. N.p., 1624.

[———.] *Sir Walter Raleigh's Ghost: or England's Forewarner. Discovering a secret Consultation, newly holden in the Court of Spain. Together with his tormenting of the Count de Gondomar; and his strange Affrightment, Confession, and publick Recantation. Laying open many Treacheries intended for the Subversion of England*. Utrecht: John Schellem, 1626.

[———.] *A Tongue-Combat, Lately Happening betweene tvvo English Souldiers in the Tilt-boat of Gravesend*. London, 1623.

[———.] *Vox Coeli, or News from Heaven. Of a Consultation there held by the high and mighty Princes, King Henry 8, King Edward 6, Prince Henry, Queene Mary, Queene Elizabeth, and Queene Anne; wherein Spaines ambition and treacheries to most Kingdomes and Free Estates in Europe, are unmasked and truly represented, but more particularly towards England, and now more especially under the pretended match of Prince Charles with the Infanta Donna Maria. Whereunto is annexed two letters written by Queene Mary from Heaven; the one to Count Gondomar, the Ambassadour of Spaine, the other to all the Roman Catholiques of England. Written by S.R.N.I. Printed in Elisium,* 1624. In *Somers Tracts,* II, 555–596.

[———.] *Vox Populi, or Newes from Spayne, translated according to the Spanish coppie, which may serve to forewarn both England and the United Provinces how farre to trust to Spanish pretences.* 1620. In *Somers Tracts,* II, 508–524.

Shakespeare, William. *Love's Labour's Lost.*

Sheavyn, Phoebe. *The Literary Profession in the Elizabethan Age.* Manchester: Manchester University Press, 1909.

Simpson, Leslie Byrd. *The Encomienda in New Spain.* Berkeley: University of California Press, 1929.

A Skeltonical Salutation or Condign Congratulation and just vexation of the Spanishe Nation, that in Bravado spent many a Crusado, in Setting forth an Armado, England to Invado. Oxford: Joseph Barnes, 1589.

The Spaniards Cruelty and Treachery to the English in the time of Peace and War Discovered. London: J. M. for Lodowick Lloyd, 1656.

Spanish Documents concerning English Voyages to the Caribbean 1527–1568. Ed. I. A. Wright. London: Hakluyt Society, ser. 2, no. 62, 1928.

Steven, William. *The History of the Scottish Church, Rotterdam.* Edinburgh: Waugh and Innes, 1832.

Strange and Wonderful Things happened to Richard Hasleton, born at Braintree in Essex, in his Ten years Travels in many foreign countries. London: A[bel] I[effes] for William Barley, 1595. In Edward Arber, *An English Garner, Voyages and Travels.* Westminister: Archibald Constable, 1903. II, 151–180.

Stow, John. *The Annales of England.* London: Ralfe Newberry, 1592.

———. *A Summary of the Chronicles of England.* London: Thomas Marshe, 1570.

Strong, Frank. "The Causes of Cromwell's West Indian Expedition," *American Historical Review,* II (1899), 228–245.

A supplication to the Kings Maiestie of Spayne, made by the Prince of Orange. Trans. out of the Dutch by T. W. London: Henry Middleton, 1573.

Taylor, E. G. R. *The Original Writings and Correspondence of the Two Richard Hakluyts.* London: Hakluyt Society, ser. 2, nos. 76–77, 1935.

[Teixeira, José.] *A Continuation of the lamentable and admirable adventures of Don Sebastian, King of Portugal, With a declaration of all his Time employed since the Battle in Africk against the Infidels, 1578, until this present year, 1603.* London: James Shaw, 1603. In *Harleian Miscellany*, II, 367–411.

[————.] *The Strangest Adventure that ever happened: either in the ages passed or present.* London: Frances Henson, 1601.

[————.] *The True History of the late and lamentable adventures of Don Sebastian, King of Portugal, after his Imprisonment in Spain until this present Day, Being now in Spain, at St. Lucar de Barrameda.* London: Simon Stafford and James Shaw, 1602. In *Harleian Miscellany*, II, 355–367.

[Thurloe, John.] *A Collection of the State Papers of John Thurloe, Esq.* Ed. Thomas Birch. 7 vols. London: 1742.

To the Right Honourable, the Knights, Citizens, and Burgesses assembled in Parliament. The Humble Petition of the Marchants Trading to the Dominions of the King of Spain. London: Joseph Moxon, 1659.

Tom Tell-Troath, or a free Discourse touching the Manners of the Time. Directed to His Majesty by waye of humble advertisement. N.d., n.p. In *Somers Tracts*, II, 469–492.

A Tragicall Historie of the troubles and Civile warres of the lowe Countries, otherwise called Flanders. Trans. Thomas Stocker. London: John Kyngston, 1583.

A Treatise against the Proclamation published by the King of Spayne by which he proscribed the late Prince of Orange. Printed in French and all other languages at Delft. N.d.

Treswell, Robert. *A Relation of such Things as were observed to happen in the Journey of the Right Honorable Charles, Earl of Nottingham, Lord High Admiral of England, his Majestys Ambassador to the King of Spain, being sent thither to take the Oath of the Said King, for the Maintenance of Peace between the two famous Kings of Great Britain and Spain, according to the several Articles formerly concluded on by the Constable of Castile, in England, in the Month of August, 1604.* Set forth by Authority. By Robt. Treswell, Esq., Somerset Herald, 1605. In *Somers Tracts*, II, 70–96.

Trevor-Davis, R. *The Golden Century of Spain.* New York: Harper and Row, 1931.

A True Discourse of the Armie which the King of Spaine caused to be assembled in the Haven of Lisbon, in the kingdome of Portugal, in the yeare 1588 against England. Trans. Daniel Archdeacon. Intro. E. B. London: John Wolfe, 1588.

A true, exact, and perfect Relation of the famous and renowned Victorie, gained by the most redoubted Armie of the mightie and victorious Monarch Philip, of that name, the fourth King of Spaine, &c. London: Samuel Browne, 1641.

A True Narrative of the late Success which it hath pleased God to give to some part of the Fleet of this Common-Wealth Upon the Spanish Coast. London: Henry Hills and John Field, printers to His Highness, 1656.

True Newes, Concerning the winning of the Towne of Corbeyll by the French King from the Prince of Parma. London: E. A., 1590.

A True Relation of a Brave English Stratagem practised lately upon a sea town in Galicia . . . as also with two other remarkable Accidents between the English and Spaniards to the glory of our Nation. Printed for Mercurius Britanicus, 1626. In *Stuart Tracts*, pp. 301–308.

A True Relation of the French King, his good successesse in winning from the Duke of Parma, his Fortes and Trenches . . . . London: John Wolfe, 1592.

A True Relation of a wonderfull Sea Fight between two great and well appointed Spanish ships or Men of Warre and a small and not very well provided English ship. N. B. [Nathaniel Butter]. 1621.

A true Report of the general Imbarrement of all the English Shippes, under dominion of the kinge of Spaine: and of the daungerous adventure and wonderfull deliuerance of a ship of London called the VIOLET. London: Thomas Wolfe for Thomas Butter, 1585.

The True Report of a great Galley that was brought unto Rochell, upon the sixt of Februarie last. London: John Wolfe, 1592.

A true Report of the lamentable Death of William of Nassawe, Prince of Orange; who was trayterouslie slayne with a Dagge, in his owne Courte, by Balthazar Serack, a Burgunion, the First of July 1584. Middelburg: Derick van Respeawe, 1584. In *Somers Tracts*, I, 407–410.

Ubaldini, Petruccio. *A Discourse concerning the Spanish Fleet Invading England in the year 1588, and Overthrown by Her Majesty's Navy under the conduct of the Right Honorable the Lord Charles Howard.* London: A. Ryther, 1590. In *Harleian Miscellany,* II, 148–166.

Underhill, John Garrett. *Spanish Literature in the England of the Tudors.* New York: Macmillan, 1899.

Ungerer, Gustav. *Anglo-Spanish Relations in Tudor Literature.* Bern: Francke Verlag, 1956.

Unwin, Rayner. *The Defeat of John Hawkins.* New York: Macmillan, 1960.

Valdes, Alfonso de. *The Sacke of Roome.* London: Abell Jesses for Roger Ward, 1590.

Verduyn, W. D. *Emanuel van Meteren.* The Hague: Martinus Nijhoff, 1926.

[Verheiden, Jacobus.] *An Oration or Speech appropriated unto the most mightie and Illustrious Princes of Christendom wherein the Right and Lawfulness of the Netherlandish Warre against Phillip King of Spain is approved and demonstrated.* Trans. Thomas Wood. N.p., 1624.

Verheyden, A. L. E. *Le Conseil des Troubles: Liste des condamnes, 1567-1573.* Brussels: Palais des Academies, 1961.

A Vision or Dreame Contayning the whole State of the Netherland warres. London: Edward Marchant, 1615.

Wadsworth, James. *The English-Spanish Pilgrime or, a New Discoverie of Spanish Popery and Iesuitical Stratagems.* Published by Authority. London: T. C. for Michael Sparke, 1630.

———. *Further Observations of the English Spanish Pilgrime Concerning Spaine.* London: Felix Kingston for Nathaniel Butter, 1630.

———. *The Present Estate of Spain.* London: A. M. for Richard Thrale and Ambrose Ritherdon, 1630.

Warner, William. *Albion's England.* London: Edm. Bollifant for George Potter, 1602.

Weldon, Sir Anthony. *The Court and Character of King James.* Pub. by Authority. London: R. J. for J. Collins, 1651. In *Secret History of the Court of James I.* 2 vols. Edinburgh: John Ballantyne, 1811.

Wernham, R. B. *Before the Armada: The Growth of English Foreign Policy, 1485-1588.* London: Jonathan Cape, 1966.

The Wicked Plots and Perfidious Practices of the Spaniards against the Seventeen Provinces of the Netherlands, before they took up Arms:

Being gathered out of several Dutch writers by a Lover of Truth, and an Unfeigned Hater of Oppression and Tyranny, the Bane of the Commonwealth. 1642. In *Harleian Miscellany*, V, 172–182.

Wiener, Leo. "Spanish Studies in England in the Sixteenth and Seventeenth Centuries," *Modern Quarterly of Language and Literature*, II (August, 1899), 3–10.

Williams, Sir Roger. *The Actions of the Low Countries.* Ed. D. W. Davies. Ithaca, N.Y.: Cornell University Press, 1964.

Williamson, J. A. *The Age of Drake.* London: Adam and Charles Black, 1938.

———. *Sir John Hawkins.* Oxford: Clarendon Press, 1927.

Willson, D. H. *King James VI and I.* London: Jonathan Cape, 1956.

Wilson, Arthur. *The History of Great Britain, being the Life and Reign of King James the First.* London: Richard Lowndes, 1653.

R[obert] W[ilson]. *The Three Lords and Three Ladies of London.* In Robert Dodsley, *A Select Collection of Old English Plays.* Ed. W. C. Hazlitt. London: Reeves and Turner, 1874–1875. VI, 371–502.

Wingfield, Anthony. *A true coppie of a discourse written by a gentleman employed in the late voyadge of Spain and Portingale.* London: T. Woodcock, 1589.

Winwood, Sir Ralph. *Memorials of the Affairs of State in the Reigns of Queen Elizabeth and King James I.* 3 vols. London: W. B. for T. Ward, 1725.

Wright, Louis B. "The Elizabethan Middle Class Taste for History," *Journal of Modern History*, III (June, 1931), 175–187.

Wright, Louis B. *Religion and Empire: The Alliance between Piety and Commerce in English Expansion, 1158-1625.* Chapel Hill, N.C.: University of North Carolina Press, 1943.

Zárate, Augustín de. *The Strange and delectable History of the discouerie and Conquest of the Provinces of Peru in the South Sea.* Trans. Thomas Nicholas. London: Richard Ihones, 1581.

Zavala, Silvio. *New Viewpoints on the Spanish Colonization of America.* Philadelphia: University of Pennsylvania Press, 1943.

———. *The Political Philosophy of the Conquest of America.* Mexico: Editorial Cultura, 1953.

INDEX

Index

Index